MEMORY'S GLASS

William Fox Conner

MEMORY'S GLASS

William Fox Conner

Illustrated by Glenn Felch

Pocahontas Press, Inc.
Blacksburg, Virginia U.S.A.

Memory's Glass by William Fox Conner, Elsah, Illinois
Cover design and illustrations by Glenn Felch, Alton, Illinois
Typesetting by Faulkner Printing, Blacksburg, Virginia
Printing and binding by Commonwealth Press, Radford, Virginia

First Printing 1995   ISBN 0-936015-53-5

Library of Congress Cataloging-in-Publication Data:
Conner, William Fox, 1940–
    Memory's glass / William Fox Conner; illustrated by Glenn
Felch.
            p. cm.
    ISBN 0-936015-53-5 (paper)
    1. Conner, William Fox, 1940–   . 2. Botetourt County (Va.)--
Biography. 3. Farm life--Virginia--Botetourt Cunty. I. Title.
CT275.C7638A3   1995   95-36729
                                                         CIP

CONTENTS

ACKNOWLEDGMENTS

I am grateful to the following publications in which several of the essays and stories have appeared:

The Christian Science Monitor: "Call Me Ishmael", "Memory's Glass", "Trading Cars", and "Taproot"

The MacGuffin: "Call Me Ishmael", "Guppies in a Gas Pump", and "Memory's Glass"

Farmer's Market: "A Promise" and "Follow Through"

The Arts Journal: "I Must Tell My Son"

Sou'wester: "Ritual"

My deepest gratitude goes to Lynn, my wife, without whose unfailing love and support my son and this book would not have been possible. A special thanks also to Jeff Rackham whose friendship, professional advice, and encouragement has been a constant source of inspiration; to Curt Martin, Abby Martin, Paula Bradley, and Norman Anderson for their willingness to read and comment on early drafts of the manuscript, and to Olivia Bertagnolli from whose inspiration I filched the title.

For Clayton

I Must Tell My Son

When I was nine,
my great-grandmother paused at dusk
to search the Virginia haze
beyond the garden. She'd
watched her father leave for war,
off across a stubble field.

Near her, in the shadows,
as I watched her eyes,
I saw him, too, a small gray figure
at the far end of a winter field,
fading into distant trees.

I should tell my son,
who played down the street
with miniatures of Star Wars figures
in a neighbor's fenced back yard,
that beyond the garden a new-cut
hayfield lay near the springhouse
where the weeping willow sank roots
through black mud.

I must tell him
before Darth Vader kills
all the rebel soldiers.

PART ONE

Memory's Glass

In my desk drawer I have one of those small daguerreotypes housed in a gilt frame and tucked into a black leather box trimmed inside with red velvet. A young woman stares out from it, but she seems to be receding into a misty background. A chemist friend of mine explained that the image is fleeing from the copper plate and that the process is irreversible.

If I look closely, however, I can make out basic features. Her hair is dark and coiffed back so that ringlets fall around her neck and shoulders. She is wearing a dark dress with what appear to be small white flowers sprinkled over it like snowflakes. Her neck and wrists are wreathed in white lace.

Her eyes are the most appealing features in her countenance. Yet they seem empty and emotionless. They appear that way partly because her image is fading and partly because I do not know who she is. I retrieved the picture a few years ago from the attic of my aunt's house the day the house was being sold at auction, but I have been unable to discover the woman's identity.

Although no memory links me to the young woman, the daguerreotype has been a curiosity to me. I have even tried to write poems about it. But because I have no emotional tie with the image it houses, a precise meaning and purpose have eluded me, like a word on the tip of my tongue that I can almost taste and feel but can't quite shape into an utterance.

Our farm lay in the Valley of Virginia, an area rich in history and strewn with artifacts. The ruins of an old plantation house lay in an overgrown lot just across the driveway from our house. It had burned several years before we moved to the farm and the remains lay in a tangle of blackberry vines, rambling rose bushes, and clumps of lilac.

I often wandered around the edges of the rubble in the first few months after we moved to the farm, peering into the darkness of the tangled undergrowth. I continued my search during the winter months, and one cold February day I found a sword buried under some bricks through which I had been probing with a long pole. At first the object I struck looked like a flat piece of metal that had fallen, probably when the chimney had collapsed during the fire. When I pried the bricks away from the side of the stone foundation, the blackened hilt of the sword appeared.

The sword was still in its scabbard when I first retrieved it, welded in by the searing heat of the fire and by the rust that had grown in it over the years. It was also slightly bent, and I managed to remove it from its housing only after a struggle. The bare blade was pitted with rust and blackened from the fire. The leather that had once formed the grip in the handle had also burned away. But for all its defects the sword fascinated me, and I wondered at it as part of an age usually cloistered in museums or locked away in attics or closets. An element of mystery attached to the sword, the kind of mystery I discovered later in the old cap-and-ball revolver that my great-grandmother kept wrapped in a shawl in her bureau drawer.

It must have been about 1948 when Granny told me about watching her father go off to war when she was still a young girl. She'd watched him wave good-bye as he walked across a stubble field. I was eight then, and she was in her nineties.

She and Nana were washing supper dishes when she told me. Her hand moved slowly, mechanically for a moment across a plate she was drying; then it stopped. She allowed her arm to fall slowly, her hand still clutching the plate, until it hung by her side like a stilled pendulum. The gold in her wire-rimmed glasses glowed faintly in the creamy evening light as she turned to stare out the front door and down across the newly-cut hayfield, trying to see back as she spoke.

In that instant she escaped the kitchen, the dishes, and the summer heat to another place and time. I remember that moment and her expression. I followed her part of the way and could see a small gray figure moving through the white mist rising from an empty field on an autumn morning. He paused at the field's distant edge, turned and waved his arm above his head, then disappeared into the trees beyond.

He didn't come back. Among the few belongings of his that remained I remember the pistol. Granny allowed me to see it from time to time. I used to be able to cock it, to pull the trigger and feel the small vibration as the hammer slammed down against the nipples on the cylinder. The pistol still had the musty smell of partly oxidized metal and aged grease.

I always wanted that pistol. I wanted to restore it, not so much as a possession but as part of the past that belonged to me. I thought I could hold the pistol and think about the figure at the far side of that field, and he wouldn't disappear into the trees.

The sword was like the pistol, except that it was a curiosity from the earth and had passed beyond belonging to anyone. I looked at it and held it up to the sky, imagining that its blade had been shiny once and might have cut the air above a horse's head in a cavalry charge. I tried to imagine it hanging by some soldier's side, an officer maybe, swaying gently to the rhythm of a horse's steady gait as a column of soldiers made its way into the haze of the upper Shenandoah. But nothing like the small, gray figure I saw when Great-grandmother spoke that evening ever appeared when I held the sword.

I have since learned that my best memories have never been housed in things. I haven't seen the pistol or the sword for years. Both of them disappeared when I was still a child, and I doubt that I could now select either of them from an accumulation of old weapons. The pistol may be restored in someone else's collection or tucked away in someone else's bureau drawer. The sword may have been carried off by some other, more avid treasure seeker.

But I still remember that summer evening when my great-grandmother looked down across that hayfield. Her image is a moment of personal history, more indelibly etched on my memory than any image tenuously captured on a copper plate. I can still remember the clear, faraway intensity in her eyes as she looked toward the small, gray figure waving at the far side of that stubble field. I can steal into that moment and wrap it around me until all the parts of it flow together and the three of us are joined like concatenated images in a long poem.

My father died in a January snow. My mother gave me his pickup truck, a fifty-two Chevrolet caked with cement dust and lots of beer cans and whiskey bottles behind the seat, and told me I would have to be the man of the house. I held that position for only two months while she made preparations to sell the farm to the Hendersons. She moved to Boston to become a Christian Science nurse. I moved into a rented room in the town of Salem, Virginia, where I attended college.

Two years later I visited the farm. Henderson had built a pond below the springhouse and leveled the fields near the railroad. The brush along the creek beds had been cleared away; the fields looked barer and longer. He'd also bulldozed the swimming pool and pushed slabs from the wall into the creeks to make solid crossings.

Paradise

My father married late, or as he explained it to my mother, he waited until he'd met the most beautiful woman in the world. For a while she took him seriously and kept herself in shape through a beauty plan requiring her to eat certain foods, take chocolate ex-lax, and spend an hour each day lying on a daybed propped up so her feet were higher than her head. Every now and then she'd ask my father or a neighbor to snap pictures of her posing in a black bathing suit. She mailed the pictures someplace as proof that she was adhering to the plan and benefiting from it. I wasn't much interested in the pictures or the plan, but I liked playing on the slanted daybed and sneaking pieces of chocolate ex-lax.

My mother cried a lot in those days. Marriage hadn't provided her the bliss and security she'd expected. My father had seen her working in Mrs. Kelsey's beauty parlor in Blacksburg. She glanced up one day in the midst of giving a permanent and saw him standing in the doorway. He smiled, stepped in among rows of chromium hair dryers and the ammonia stench of neutralizer, and asked her out. He was gentlemanly, opening doors and holding chairs for her. He handed her into cars and walked on the outside when they strolled down the street. He even took her by the elbow when they crossed through traffic. She thought him chivalrous. "He was the first man to treat me like a lady," she once told me. Besides, he came from a good family: his father had been a professor of mechanical engineering at V.P.I., and his

9

mother, a kindly, subservient woman, had taught piano and painted still life.

My father courted my mother one month before asking her to marry him. Suddenly, a brief legal agreement, conducted by a justice of the peace without ceremony at the local courthouse, linked my mother to a man she could never be quite sure of, in a marriage that was like a long dialogue between the flesh and the spirit.

She soon discovered an undercurrent of crudeness in him. He tended to be selfish, had an uncontrollable temper, and indulged himself with bootleg whiskey or store-bought spirits. When he was drunk his temper flared to brute rage. He never struck her, but he broke furniture; and once rammed his fist through a wall in a fit of anger.

Deeply concerned for her soul, my mother read her Bible daily and attempted to practice a Christian life. At least once she took me to a Communion service, but wouldn't allow me to taste the purple juice from the tray of shiny glasses because I wasn't old enough to understand. The tray smelled faintly like Grapette, my favorite soft drink, as it passed by in a flourish of hands and arms. Folks plucked the thimble-sized glasses from their sockets and quaffed the liquid in one gulp the way my father drank whiskey from the small glasses he called jiggers.

My mother found little solace in her prayers. Simple faith could not fill the emptiness in her marriage, or make up for her earlier failure at a singing career, or calm her fears of a global war that made rationing a way of life and conjured up the worst of biblical prophecies. She stopped exercising. Snapshots in the years after the war show a plump woman smiling with her children or among groups of relatives.

My father worked as an electrician for the Newport News Ship Building and Dry Dock Company, or as he called it, "the shipyard." One or two remaining photographs show him in dark pleated dress pants and a white shirt with the sleeves rolled tightly around the muscles in his upper arms. He was barrel-chested and stocky, standing only five feet, eight inches. His legs were slightly bowed and so muscular they appeared gnarled. His arms were unusually long for a man his size and extremely powerful. He often quoted Housman's poem about an athlete dying young and liked the lines, "Smart lad, to slip betimes away / From fields where glory does not stay." Sometimes, after reciting the lines, he'd smile, lock his hands around a small tree or metal post and leverage himself straight out.

In the years before he married my mother he'd prided himself on his athletic prowess. He boxed for a while, until an opponent broke his nose. He doggedly pursued tennis, even built a dirt court on a side lot near the house in Blacksburg where he'd grown up, but abandoned the game to take a job as a driver for a wealthy man in town.

The new job provided opportunities for him to develop his golf game, and he must have flirted with the idea of turning pro. Then he played a few holes with a kid named Sam Snead, he said, at The Homestead in Hot Springs; the trouncing must have demoralized him. He recalled the experience with awe and melancholy as though a chance for fortune and dignity had slipped from his grasp.

He also loved baseball and played a few months with a New York Yankee farm team somewhere in the Caroli-

11

nas. The only story he ever told me about that part of his life concerned the day he first tried chewing tobacco. He was playing in the outfield, chewing and swallowing the juice; "I got dizzy," he'd begin. "The whole field started spinning. Then the fly ball went straight over my head. I began backing up, trying to keep my eyes on the ball, but that thing turned fuzzy, split into three or four balls and I couldn't stop. I fell, swallowed the chew, and spent the next day in bed." He'd laugh as he told the end of the story, pointing upward as though the ball were still in the air.

At the age of thirty-six he married my mother. Two months later he went to Chicago to take a six-month course in the applications of electricity. He returned with a thick heavy book bound in dark leather. Its smudged gray pages felt gritty and contained electrical diagrams drawn in thin gray lines. From Chicago he moved to Newport News and the shipyard. He continued to keep himself in shape playing catch or chipping golf balls with neighbors in a vacant lot across the street from our apartment in Raleigh Court.

During his years with the shipyard I didn't see him much, but one afternoon my mother and I rode the bus to meet him when he got off work. He walked up a ramp out of a maze of iron pipes, steel cables and girders as colorless and dense as the diagrams in his book. All around the air hissed and clattered in a roar of metal and engines and tall cranes pawing the air like giant mosquitoes.

On a winter day my father came home on crutches and stayed at home for several days. He looked pained and quiet. He'd been on a ship that was finished except for a few details. The ship had been launched while my father was still on it, a common practice during war time. The civilian workmen were supposed to stay with the vessel until it docked later. But my father never did a thing he didn't want to do. As the ship left the dock, he jumped off and broke his ankle.

For a while we lived on a farm owned by a man named Turner. He had a Caterpillar tractor, and Malcolm, his hired man, sometimes let me ride with him. The tractor rumbled, turning in jerks and squeaks between its two cleated steel tracks. I could feel the throb of its engine through the steel floor plates and smooth black seat. The machine rocked like a boat as it crawled over the ridges between the rows of trees in Mr. Turner's orchard. I liked the smell of metal and gasoline and grease mixed with the scent of dust from the fields.

During our stay at the Turner farm, my parents argued. "We can't stay here!" she'd say. "We can't raise children on a farm worker's pay."

"So what do you want me to do, dammit?" He hadn't liked working in the shipyard. He never really liked working for someone else; for a couple of years he'd tried to run a small business in Blacksburg, repairing radios and small appliances. He called it the Fix-All Shop. But he preferred drinking, fishing in the summer and hunting in the fall, to the tedium of broken toaster filaments and burned-out radio tubes. He fared a little better as a projectionist at one of the local theaters; ultimately, he would always need the stability of a paycheck from someone else. "Look, I keep telling you, this is just temporary," he'd say, finally, and leave the house, his heavy work shoes thudding on the wooden porch boards and steps.

When he wasn't working, my father walked the land. I climbed the hills with him sometimes, but most often he went off alone. "What's he looking for?" I once asked my mother after he'd left the house.

"Maybe paradise, at least a way out," she replied, "but he won't find it out there." She watched him walk down a dirt road toward a patch of woods behind a packing shed. "Besides, he's a hunter; he's always looking for something. I wonder if you'll be the same way."

"A farm is the only way to live," my father said to my mother one morning. "It's a simpler life." Mother and I had taken up residence with Grandaddy and Nana who lived in Starkey, just south of Roanoke. My father had been in and out. Then one day a man in a big black car drove us out to a farm near Troutville. The place was owned by a man named I. O. Bower. Even years after we'd moved, my father relished saying, "I owe Bower; I surely do."

Ours was a working dairy farm, a rectangular piece of ground comprising one hundred and thirty-six acres. Route 779 marked its northern boundary. Its southern border ran a hundred yards beyond the crest of Tinker Mountain, which rose like a steep wall along the back side of the farm. The Henderson farm, a well-kept place with rolling green hills, connected with ours to the west; to the east lay a rugged and poorly-tended place occupied by a man named Henry Booth.

A team of mules, Jake and Rhody, came with the farm, and horse-drawn machinery with names you could hold in your mouth the way my father explained that spring water should be tasted: "Don't swallow it so quickly; roll it around in your mouth; chew it." He'd take a careful drink, work his mouth around, then sluice the water noisily down his throat. "Most satisfying drink in the world," he'd say. I learned that the long cutting arm of a mowing machine was a sickle bar with guards and sections and a grassboard on the end. A pitman rod underneath the machine drove the sickle back and forth as the wheels turned. Bottom plows consisted of moldboards, shares, beams, and colters. A hand-held mowing scythe could be fitted with a grass blade or a briar hook by means of a tang. The curved handle was a snath. My father harnessed the mules with collars, hames, cruppers, girths, traces and trace chains. These latter he hooked to singletrees, which fastened to doubletrees. In a few years when he bought a tractor, he hooked the shortened tongue of the trailer to the drawbar on the tractor with a clevis and drawbar pin. He raked hay into windrows with a dump rake, then shocked it in the field until it could be hauled and stacked in mows in the barn. He cut wheat and corn with binders, pulled by horses and later by tractors; wide, cleated bull wheels drove the mechanisms that cut and tied the wheat into sheaves, the corn into bundles. Threshed wheat left straw, and a smaller residue called chaff; corn was shucked, then shelled, leaving empty cobs and fodder.

"Haw, now. Haw, now. Gee a little. Gee a little," he sang out to Rhody as she pulled the three-footed plow between rows of six-inch corn. He'd loop one end of the long rein over his right shoulder so he could guide the plow with both hands while guiding the mule with his voice. "Best single-line animal I've ever worked," he'd boast. "Why, she can walk, she can talk, she can crawl on her belly like a reptile." He'd smile and do a little hootchy-kootchy in the corn rows. "That's good mountain air," he say when the mule farted and the aroma wafted back over him.

The air in Newport News had been coal dust from the bin just outside our front door and diesel fumes from the bus as it rocked away from my mother and me on the uneven two-lane road in the country near Aunt Grace's house. Acrid winds blowing across Raleigh Court from the shipyard mingled with the smells of fried potatoes and the oily smell of fish in the evenings. Summer nights stayed hot and damp.

The farm cooled at night. Breezes blew off Tinker Mountain, and we slept under light blankets. During the day the sun drew grass and weed smells from the fields. I chewed and swallowed the names: ragweed, bluegrass, timothy, broom sedge, orchard grass, fescue, goldenrod, sour grass, alfalfa, lespedeza, clover. The hollow rising toward the mountain behind the barns smelled of decaying leaves. Hay mows in the big barn were high and airy with the light, dusky aroma of hay. The stable area below held the acid-sweet odor of manure. Sour milk tainted the air of the ten-stanchioned milking barn, even though my father washed the concrete floor daily with a hose. The attached red silo held the rancid smell of fermented silage. A stinging, chemical odor of disinfectant soap lingered in the milk house, a small building made of cinder blocks and containing a cooler and milking equip ment—ten-gallon cans, five-gallon stainless steel milking pots, suction cups, and rubber hoses arranged on metal racks.

Mottled black and white cows with names like Blackie, Tilly, Flora Artis, Mona and Popeye gathered near the barn at milking time. Their breaths smelled of chewed pasture; their warm milk which my father often

16

sampled from a stripping cup tasted foamy and sweet. The cows smelled different from the mules or pigs, or the heavy reek of the chickens that Nana raised in a coop behind her house. A musky odor of dried grain and mouse pee pervaded the empty corn crib and the dark bins of the granary.

A truck came with the farm. I.O. Bower owned a fuel oil business and had removed the tank from a well-used, snub-nosed, 1940 Chevrolet two-ton truck and replaced it with a flat bed. We didn't have an automobile when we moved to the farm, so the truck served both as farm vehicle and family car. A faint scent of fuel oil lingered in its floor mat and in the horse hair spilling from rips in its seat.

Grandaddy and Nana moved into the larger of the two houses on the farm. It was white clapboard with a tin roof and sat on a low hill a quarter of a mile north of the barns.

Our house, two rooms and a screened porch under a tar paper roof and protected by whitewashed wood siding, had been built as a summer place more or less in the center of the farm. It rested near an outcropping of shale in a small valley between the barns and the second house. The screened porch side of the house opened onto a wide yard. Long whitewashed benches, a picnic table built around a small weeping willow tree, and a stone barbecue pit sat on the left side of the yard. A play-house, large enough for children to walk into and roughly the shape of a colonial mansion, complete with shake shingles and a porch with supporting columns, stood against a fence near the left side of the house. Just beyond the toy mansion, all along the eastern edge of the yard, the sun sparkled across the waters of a swimming pool.

A small bathhouse stood to the right of the summer house, a few feet back from the pool's shallow end.

The pool was not fancy. It was in fact little more than a concrete dam across a low place. A thin, uneven layer of concrete, poured over the irregular contours of the ground sloping toward the dam, formed the bottom. According to the date carved in the top of the wall the pool had been constructed in 1941. To get around a shortage of materials, the builders had not reinforced the concrete and had mixed the cement with common creek sand to give it bulk. The entire pool was porous and full of cracks, and the area behind it became a swamp when the pool was full. Young willow trees flourished in the primal ooze, and on hot days cows escaping summer flies among the willows made sucking sounds as they waded through the muck.

I liked the pool. My aunts and uncles brought my cousins, and we swam for hours and there were picnics with lots of food: hamburgers or hot dogs with home-made chili, potato salad, baked beans, and deviled eggs. Corn on the cob, sliced tomatoes and cucumbers appeared straight from the garden. Usually, the relatives arrived in their cars, but at least once my father drove the truck into Roanoke and hauled them out to the farm. I sat on the pool dam one Saturday afternoon watching for them. The truck was loud because of a shot muffler, so I could hear it long before I saw the heads and arms of my aunts and uncles and cousins above the cattle frames when the truck appeared through the locust and persimmon trees bordering the road.

My father referred to all the relatives on my mother's side as "the rabble," but he secretly enjoyed squiring them out to the farm in the truck. Sitting in the cab he was higher than anything else on the road, and if he shifted down to the lowest gear, which he called "Granny," the truck was all but unstoppable, even when he extended the bed eight feet and loaded the truck with loose hay until it crawled along like a beetle, the cab barely visible under the load.

He liked the pool, too; it suited his notion of paradise. He'd walk along the top of the dam holding his stomach in and his chest out like a banty rooster. He liked swimming late in the evening, especially if the water was cold. "Come on in, the water's fine," he'd call out, and turn red laughing when my mother or one of the relatives jumped in and came up sputtering and shivering in the night air. They seemed never to doubt him.

The pool also troubled him. When we first moved to the farm the pool filled through a rusty inch-and-a-half pipe stretching from the shallow end around the side of the house and up a hollow to a small creek. The creek ran from a spring near the foot of Tinker Mountain and down through Henderson's pasture, before entering our place. The fill pipe had simply been placed so that one end of it siphoned water from a deep place in the creek. From that point the pipe stretched along the ground like a long brown snake. Someone once asked my father if the water in the pool was clean enough to swim in. "Clean!" he quipped sharply; "Why hell, Man, it's pasturized."

Bower told my father that it took forty days to fill the pool. Forty days seemed a long time, and in the summer heat and frequent droughts water leaked from the pool slightly faster than it came in. During the summer of our first year the water level subsided until the pool stood half empty. My father shook his head as he watched the slow trickle of water from the end of the small fill pipe.

Then he took a surveyor's hand level and made sightings along the creeks that ran from the hollows on both sides of the pool. Near the foot of Tinker Mountain an army of small pine trees sprouted among clumps of broomsedge in the pasture. "We're going to have to mow this ground soon," my father remarked one morning as we rounded up the cattle to drive them down to the milking barn. But no one mowed it because my father got too busy plotting ways to siphon more water from the creeks into the pool.

"Mallee"

Grandaddy Douthat was a large man, over six feet, with a bald head and thick glasses. He wore a wide-brimmed felt hat, even when he walked in his yard. He dressed in long-sleeved work shirts and suspenders to hold up his gray trousers that hung to the rims of his brown high-topped shoes, the kind with hooks instead of eyes for the laces. He always kept them clean and polished. He'd been a railroad man for half a century, and all those years had so hardened him that he was uncomfortable around women and children. He spoke with a loud voice, and I tried to keep my distance when he was in the house.

For at least thirty years he worked as an engineer for the Virginian and later for the Norfolk and Western. He thought The Powhatan Arrow was a fast train and seemed to like saying the name as much as I enjoyed hearing it. "The Powhatan Arrow," he'd say, drawing the name out and smacking his lips as if he might have been tasting the smoke from its stack, and I imagined a streamliner rushing down a long straight track with smoke roiling back over it in a long plume.

In his last years with the Norfolk and Western, Grandaddy'd hauled coal from Mullens, West Virginia, to Roanoke. He sometimes mentioned his "Mallee," which I later learned was a locomotive designed originally in the later nineteenth century by a Swiss engineer named Anatole Mallet. Grandaddy'd pronounce the name "Mallee." In her later years Nana often spoke with pride of Grandaddy's being the first man to drive a diesel locomotive into Roanoke. She kept a picture of him and his crew carefully posed by a massive engine with six drive wheels rising nearly to each man's shoulders. Grandaddy was standing in the front row wearing his wide brimmed hat and wire-rimmed glasses, the gold chain of his railroad watch suspended in a loop from the pocket of his black vest. Some of the men were smiling, but Grandaddy wore a sober, almost puzzled expression.

After his retirement Grandaddy hadn't found much to do before we all moved to the farm. He walked in his yard in Starkey with his hands in his pockets, as if he were looking for something, but had forgotten what it was or where he'd left it. He often sat in the glider on the front porch staring out across the neighborhood. Every now and then he'd shift his weight in the glider, draw a deep breath, then release it, half sighing, half moaning "Lordy, Lordy, Lordy" to himself in the escape of breath. Sometimes in the evening we'd hear a train in the distance and when its whistle blew he'd smile and call it by number and say where it was going.

Taproot

My mother read her Bible daily and quoted from it often. For her the stories were real. An innocent among works of literature, she read her Bible as a testament to the trials and expectations of man, and strove to live righteously in an alien world of financial and domestic frustrations. She had a missionary zeal to give of herself. "I admire good relations among folks," she once told me, and her religion taught her that "all things were possible in the sight of God," and that her moral freedom was "a God-given right." On the farm she worked under the pressure of seasons, traditions, machinery, constantly accumulating dust and the ebb and flow of my father's moods.

"Evil is not real," she declared, sometimes half aloud to me, but mainly to herself, "and you don't have to give in to it, in no way and under no condition." She fought invisible forces and saw signs in temperature changes and in the vagaries of human behavior. Intuitively, she struggled against foes that the rest of the family couldn't see, or were not ready to accept. To counteract uncertainties she prayed daily and worked, canning and preserving vegetables and fruits throughout the summer, and cleaning her house assiduously all year long. Later, to help out with the family income, she went back to the beauty business, a vocation she'd abandoned shortly after her marriage, and opened a beauty parlor in Daleville.

"**W**ell, Woman," my father said to my mother one day in early summer of our second year on the farm. "Think you can stir up enough food to stuff a threshing crew? They'll be coming in a week." The previous fall he'd planted his first crop of winter wheat to help provide for the hogs and dairy herd.

My mother looked surprised for a moment as though she had not expected to be asked to take on such a load. "Well, yes," she replied, finally. "What kinds of things should I fix?"

"Meat and potatoes. Stuff that'll stick to your ribs, and lots of iced tea," he told her.

Gentle, contemplative, and city-bred, my mother failed to see the farm as a paradise. But she was industrious and possessed a desire to please that was like a taproot probing deep into hidden streams. She commenced her preparations for the meal days in advance. She'd give them lots of iced tea, sliced ham and fried chicken, as well as mashed potatoes, brown beans and corn bread. There'd be homemade biscuits, too, and apple pie for dessert. She determined they'd leave stuffed to their throats.

For my mother the amount of food a guest ate in her house measured her success as a hostess. A person eating moderately at her table drew sidelong glances and risked offending her as a refusal to dine might offend a tribal leader. To my father's consternation she often insisted that visiting relatives or friends depart with gallons of milk, pint or quart jars filled with pure cream, or pounds of home-churned butter.

"Dammit, Woman, I'm not running a dairy farm to keep your people in milk and butter!" he'd shout, stomping around the kitchen after the last car had disappeared down our lane late on a Sunday afternoon.

"Oh, we'll never miss a little milk and butter; we have plenty."

"Well, when we have to move to the poorhouse, I'll never say I told you so."

The threshers arrived in late June. The threshing machine, with its steel spoked wheels, lumbered ponderously up the driveway behind 'Am Elbert's Case tractor. The sound of the tractor muffled to a steady purr against the clatter and rumble of the threshing machine. It barely fit through the opening of the big barn and stood like a colossus between the two hay mows. A long belt in a skinny figure eight stretched from a pulley on the machine through the entryway to a pulley on the tractor.

Threshing was a community event. 'Am Elbert, the owner of the equipment, was a Dunker, a member of the Old Order of the Brethren Church, or "Old Ordy Brethren," as some folk referred to the persuasion. Dunkers believed in hard work and some abstinence from materialism. They drove black cars and dressed simply—the men in bibbed denim overalls and black, wide-brimmed hats, the women in plain blue or gray dresses with black bonnets and shoes. Their religious teaching apparently forbade modern conveniences in the home, but allowed for an abundance of farm machinery. So, while the women cooked, washed, and sewed with woodstoves, tubs and needles, the men plowed, planted, and harvested with all the latest farm equipment.

'Am appeared to be the one man in the community who could afford large machines, and he custom farmed, plowing, baling hay, and threshing for other farmers, many of whom had not completed the transition from horses to tractors. Just after the war, farm machinery was too dear to be bought easily. Most people just made do by converting horse-drawn machinery. They removed long tongues, singletrees and doubletrees from drills, cultivators, manure spreaders, wagons, and even plows, and replaced them with shorter tongues and hitches to fit drawbars on tractors.

So shortly after eight o'clock that morning, 'Am started the Case tractor and engaged the pulley and belt leading to the threshing machine. "Let 'er rip!" my father yelled from the top of the first load of unthreshed wheat.

The machine worked mysteriously. Sheaves of grain which had been cut in the field by a binder, collected into shocks then hauled to the barn on trucks or wagons pulled by tractors or teams of mules and horses, were untied and tossed into one end of the machine as fast as men could work. A hum flowed steadily from the threshing machine. Thin wisps of dust sifted through cracks in its galvanized metal sides and from around gear housings, permeating the air from the threshing floor to the eaves of the barn roof. The cleaned wheat appeared at a small opening in the side of the machine and spilled into waiting burlap sacks. Straw and chaff, to be used later for bedding, shot out the end of the long boom at the rear.

'Am, nicknamed from Sam because his father had a harelip and couldn't pronounce the first letter of his son's name, worked along with the other men, but more resolutely, steadily and quietly. A shy, easy-going man, he didn't practice the banter enjoyed by the other farmers. He smiled often, although sometimes, if you watched him closely when he was going real hard, the expression seemed to lock into place and become sinister.

While threshing, 'Am hovered around his machinery like an anxious mother, listening to it, making adjustments. He worked with cat-like movements, reaching gingerly through belts and pulleys, unclogging vents and chutes, moving levers, or checking grain sacks. Periodically he'd apply a stick of pine rosin to the underside of the moving belt to keep it from slipping. 'Am worked with the sure-footed ease of a man used to being around machinery, but over the years his machines had exacted a toll.

Neighbors told the story that one day while baling hay 'Am stopped to correct a malfunction near the big flywheel at the side of his International baler. The wheel snapped his middle finger between it and the belt, clipping off the end of his finger near the first knuckle. "Shit," 'Am muttered, shaking the blood off the stub. He examined the damage for a moment, then wrapped his hand in his blue bandana handkerchief and continued his work. By the age of thirty-five he carried only one or two undamaged fingers on each hand. "We all sacrifice a little to machinery," my father observed as he watched 'Am baling hay in the field below the house. "It seems the bigger, fancier and more powerful the machines the more we give up."

In the early morning I rode one of the wagons to the field and watched the men load shocks of grain for a while, then rode back on one of the loads. I hung around the threshing machine, watching 'Am, until my father sent me to carry water from the milk barn to the threshing crew. The granary lay on the left side of the entryway to the barn, just a few steps from where the threshed grain poured into waiting sacks. With the steady flow the grain bins began to fill quickly, and just before noon I crawled to the top of a full one and curled down into the warm wheat.

In the main barn machinery roared. The joint in the long belt slapped rhythmically against the pulleys on the threshing machine and the tractor. The tractor engine labored and eased in the rhythm of the grain flow as the feeders tossed in unbound sheaves and reached for new ones. Voices bounced along on top of the roar, sometimes rising high above it in shouts, then subsiding back into it. Then everything went quiet.

When I awakened the machinery had been shut down. The barn roof popped in the midday heat. A cow resting in a stable beneath coughed. Another groaned as she belched up more cud to be chewed. Pigeons flapped and cooed in the eaves. Outside crickets chirred in the grass, and the Case tractor stood in the shade of a pecan tree, emitting metallic clicks and pings from its cooling engine.

The house, too, was quiet as the men ate lunch. They seemed out of place in the kitchen. My mother hovered around the table, offering extra helpings as each man cleaned his plate. She'd been nervous at the thought of feeding fifteen men, but as the meal progressed she lost her fear and simply worked. She was a dancer in the midst of her long-awaited performance, an actor captivated by her role.

She piled each plate with corn bread, beans and mashed potatoes. Thick ham steaks hung over the edges of plates. She placed a bowl of biscuits in the center of the table and a platter of fried chicken at each end. A pitcher of newly churned buttermilk with flecks of yellow in it sat on the counter near a four-gallon crock of iced tea, and she'd prepared coffee for the men who didn't mind the extra heat. For dessert she served apple and cherry pies sliced into quarters and buried under scoops of ice cream.

The men spoke quietly, perhaps a little stunned by the volume of food. They thanked my mother as she served extra helpings of meat, bread, and potatoes, or poured more iced tea and coffee, but they didn't banter as they had in the field or in the barn. They ate steadily, almost hurriedly.

At the table 'Am Elbert removed his wide-brimmed hat. His hair lay straight and tight against his head where his hat had sweated it into place. Below the hat line the ends of his hair curled upward in a monk's fringe around the sides and back of his head. He kept his blue, long-sleeved shirt tightly buttoned at his throat and cuffs. He ate the way he worked, quietly and assiduously, like a priest carrying out a sacred rite.

"Thank you, Ma'am," he said politely, rising from the table even as he laid down the fork after a last bite. He was the first to leave. He made his move quickly, passing from the kitchen through the living room, where he swept up his hat and pressed it on his head in a single move as he lunged out the front door.

"You're welcome, Sam," my mother said as 'Am fled down the porch steps. She stood transfixed in the kitchen doorway for a moment; then, waving a fly away from her face, or banishing the smell of grease and sweat, she turned back to the rest of the busily eating men.

It burst from the glare of the morning sun and bore down on us, a dark form, roaring, its engine wide open, its broad cleated tires gouging hash marks into the pavement.

"What the hell!" my father exclaimed, raising his hand to shade his eyes against the bright light as the loud form came into view — a combine, red with its reel and sickle teeth jutting out in front like a gaping mouth. High in the glassed-in cab, 'Am Elbert gripped the steering wheel and smiled as he guided the new machine past us, waving distractedly, heading west up 779, the machine steady and heavy on the road

"Well, times are changing," my father observed. He pulled the mail from the silver box by the road as the combine disappeared over the hill, then climbed into the pickup. "We'd better go; your mother'll be waiting lunch on us," he said. We could see her in the distance, a small figure in the yard at the back of the house, one hand on her hip, the other shading her eyes, watching us, like a pioneer woman studying movement far across the prairie.

The Peeny-Weeny Man

My sister, Betty, was barely walking when we moved to the farm. By the age of two she had blue eyes, skinny legs, and hair the color of unripened corn silk. Once while sleeping bare-bottomed on my father's chest as he lay on the living room floor, listening to "Amos 'n Andy," she peed on him. The baptism bound him to her, and she governed him with a force as ancient as the earth itself, but which had nothing to do with size or brute strength. A tug from her hand could cool his rage, warm him on cold days, or cheer him on blue ones. She was essence and frailty above the hardness of responsibilities. He was a child at heart and needed the contact.

He bantered with her. "May I do anything for you, Princess?" he'd ask, kneeling to her as she sat on the sofa, smiling.

"Yes, you may bring me my doll and change her dress." He'd feign reluctance.

"No, I think you should get your doll, Princess. Couldn't you get your doll?" Then he'd wait for her response, knowing what it would be.

"Daddy!" She'd raise her voice to a commanding pitch. "If you don't bring my doll I'm going to go off with the Penny-Weeny man, and heaven will come and die you."

A salesman from Ralston Purina had made a number of trips to sell my father new brands of feed and calf starter. My sister had been impressed with the man, especially his truck with red and white checkerboards on its doors.

"Oh, please don't go off with the Peeny-Weeny man," my father would plead earnestly. "I'll get your doll." He'd run into the bedroom and bring the doll and proceed to dress it, the rough skin of his hands raking against the soft cloth. Then he'd hand the crudely attired doll to her. "Here you are, Princess. Will there be anything more?" Usually she had no more requests. She seemed to know that the game should be carried only so far.

Later she developed the powerful weapon of the raised forefinger. She'd give him an order which he'd ignore, or he'd indicate that he was too busy to play or meet her request. She's raise her voice to a command and hold up her finger for emphasis. He could never resist the gesture, even in times of real anger. "Oh Lord, Child, I don't want to play now," he'd complain, but even as he spoke the lines in his face would soften. "Come on, Sweetie, let's not play now," he'd whine. But under her spell he was helpless. "Oh dammit," he'd finally say, partly in disgust at his own weakness and partly at the power of her charm which always amused and subdued him.

Over the years as my father grew more and more reclusive and more uncontrollable in his drinking, the relationship between him and my sister never wavered. Her voice was summer dawn in the heat of tension or in the dark of winter. Watching them, I began to understand that fathers are clay before such diminutive women in whose eyes they see child, demon, lover, friend, and immaculate mother.

When the train blew through the town of Troutville ten miles away we could hear it only faintly on regular days and even then you had to be listening for it. On cold days when the sky turned gray and heavy the train whistle came clear and sharp as if it were only just across the hill from our place. "It's gonna snow," my father would say. "You can feel it in the air." Far away you could hear the train rushing through Troutville like a great storm heading toward Cloverdale and Roanoke.

Snow

"Give me five minutes more, only five minutes more," my father's voice boomed out on those summer mornings of 1948 as he climbed the hill to the milk barn. "Let me stay, let me stay in your arms." From his front porch a quarter of a mile away Grandaddy sang in reply: "Give me five minutes more, only five minutes more." Then he'd laugh and look at Nana and say, "That man's crazy. What you gwine do wit him?"

The summer heat abated, and in the early fall my father decided to pipe water to our house. Grandaddy and Nana's house had water, supplied by a tall spigot with a lever on top that you could flip back and forth and get water, but you had to wait a couple of seconds as the spigot hissed and gurgled the water from ground level to its spout. Best of all was the thunking sound and the vibration in the spigot when you flipped the lever repeatedly off and on but slowly enough to keep the water halfway up the long stem. I imagined the vibrations extending all the way to the spring box at the foot of the mountain.

Grandaddy watched as my father and Theodore Dove laid the three-quarter-inch galvanized pipe in the newly dug trench running from the milk house to the side of our house. Dove, as we called him, a small, wiry man with sandy hair, blue eyes, and bronzed complexion, had come to live with us after leaving the army, because he had no place to go. My father had met him in Blacksburg and had taken him in like a brother or a son.

Dove didn't talk much about the war. My father said he'd been an infantry soldier in the Battle of the Bulge and had lost a lot of friends. Dove once told me that he'd chased a German soldier across a ridge, firing at him with a machine gun, but never hitting him. He spoke very slowly with a hint of a smile on his lips.

"Did you like the war?" I once asked him.

"Not when my friends died," he said.

Dove was quiet, except when he worked with my father. They kept up a running banter along the trench, and invented their own language for the task.

"Where's de gleeple?" my father would say to Dove.

"Rat here," he'd reply and hand him a coupler or an elbow.

"Now we need some glop for de gleeple. Where's de glop?"

"Rat here," and Dove would hand him a tube of Permatex.

"Them boys is crazy, just plain crazy," Grandaddy groaned, willing, but not quite able, to enter into the banter and horseplay.

He liked helping out on the farm, but all those years of yelling at his fireman over the roar and clatter of laboring steam locomotives had given his voice the power of a bull horn, and life around heavy machinery had deprived him of humor and made him suspicious of all gentleness. He loved my grandmother, a slight woman only half his size. She'd borne him nine children, seven of whom survived, but the closest he ever came to an open display of affection for her was when one of the relatives asked him to pose for a picture with Nana. Grandaddy could make himself pose only if he joked about it. He'd lay his arm across Nana's shoulders and say, "Miss Laura, you're a good ol' gal."

He also laughed at my sister, who was only two when we moved to the farm, because he thought she was clumsy. She seemed forever tripping over his sprawled out legs. He'd never bother to move them; he'd just smile up at my mother, his favorite of all his own children, and say, "Evelyn, I do believe that's the clumsiest child I've even seen."

"Well, you could move your feet, Dad." She always spoke gently to Grandaddy and never got angry with him.

Grandaddy'd laugh way down in his stomach and never move an inch.

When he drove the mules he bawled at them, swearing and urging them on the way he might have urged his "Mallee" engine up steep grades out of the mountains around Mullens, West Virginia, and down the Valley of Virginia, trying to make it to Roanoke on time.

He knew about time and railroad schedules. He'd hear trains passing through Troutville and often know where they'd come from — the 8:10 out of Winchester, or the 12:05 out of D.C. He'd retired from the railroad but had never given it up.

"He'll kill them, dammit," my father muttered one day as we watched Grandaddy mowing lespedeza in the long, ten acre field that stretched along Route 779. At the far end of the field, a quarter of a mile away, Grandaddy yelled and shook the reins, pushing the mules to the top of the hill. He turned them and came toward us, slapping the reins and yelling relentlessly, "Get on mules! Get on! Yah! Yah!" until the mules, lathered with white foam, broke into a trot trying to get away from the voice filing at them like rasp.

He jerked the laboring animals to a halt a few feet from where we were standing. The sweaty harness leather creaked rhythmically and the mowing machine jerked back and forth in the motion of their breathing.

"What the hell's your rush?" I'd never heard my father speak that sharply to him. Grandaddy sat still on the mowing machine and looked straight at my father, but he didn't speak. My father was angry beyond caring what Grandaddy thought. He had a soft place for animals and didn't like to see them abused.

"Get off!" He stepped to the rear of the mowing machine and snatched the reins from Grandaddy's hands.

"I can handle them," Grandaddy said, but all the power had drained from his voice.

"Like hell you can, Old Man," my father replied. "They aren't machines. Look at them. You've probably winded them. They won't be worth a damn for any-thing." He draped the reins around the brass horn on the hame of Jake's collar and unhooked both mules from the mower.

Grandaddy slid from the pancake seat and began walking toward the house, shuffling through the opening in the honeysuckle along the edge of the field and up the gravel driveway, dulling the shine on his high-topped shoes.

"Grandaddy's sick," my mother told me one morn-ing. "You'd better not plan to go up for breakfast." She looked worried, but that wasn't unusual. My mother frequently wore an anxious look when she was busy. Her voice sounded tighter than usual so I decided not to go up to Nana's house that morning. Grandaddy and Nana always served salt-rising bread for breakfast and I had made a habit of having a piece of toast or two with them in the mornings. Salt-rising bread with freshly churned buttermilk had become my favorite breakfast.

Several days passed and I was still not allowed to go up to Nana's house. By then I knew something was seriously wrong. Aunts and uncles arrived from Roanoke without my cousins and spoke to me distractedly. Mostly, they stayed up at Nana's house. Sometimes they'd walk down to our house late at night and talk quietly in the kitchen.

"I think he's worse," I heard my mother say one night. "Doctor Davis doesn't think he can do any more for him." Her voice had a sadness in it, the kind I'd heard before when we lived in Newport News. She hadn't sounded that way on the farm. She hadn't even cried in the two years we'd lived there. Much of her summer had been taken up by her garden and making preserves, blackberry, strawberry, raspberry. She'd canned sour cherries for pies, churned butter, and fed the threshing crew when they harvested our wheat. She'd had little time to cry.

"The doctors don't know what to do," my father said. His voice sounded hard. He hadn't been to a doctor since he was a child and had almost died of scarlet fever. He had little use for doctors. "Hell, they scared him into being sick when they told him he had a bad heart. He was never well after that. They made him sick."

The conversation got quiet. Someone sobbed, and I could hear a spoon ringing against the sides of a coffee cup.

"Well, Doctor Davis has been the family doctor for years and Momma trusts him," I heard my mother say with a slight edge in her voice. He's doing everything he can."

"Poor Daddy," someone said.

"The Peeny-Weeny man," my father said, apparently speaking to no one in particular.

"What?"

"The Peeny-Weeny man," my father said again.

"It's what Betty calls the Purina man," my mother said. "She keeps telling Bill she'll run off with him. It's her threat to keep her daddy in the palm of her hand."

"Children," someone said and laughed quietly. A spoon rang against a coffee cup. The flue cover above my bed whistled softly as the wind drew through the stove in the other room.

A day or so later my mother asked me if I wanted to see Grandaddy. I wasn't sure. I'd always been a little afraid of him. He was an imposing man in both size and voice, and around him I felt out of place and uncomfortable. He'd poked fun at my sister when she tripped over his feet, and he teased me when I ate more than two pieces of salt-rising toast. I wasn't sure he liked children. So I didn't know what to think about seeing him. I knew he'd be different, but I wasn't sure why or how. My mother took me up to Nana's house anyway. Everyone was quiet there.

"Grandaddy's in the bedroom," she said as she led me through the door. The room was dark because the shades were drawn. Grandaddy lay under a large, plastic canopy. He looked small and withered. A green tank, like those I'd seen in Mr. Dooley's blacksmith shop, stood near the head of the bed. I'd never seen Grandaddy so quiet.

"Dad?" my mother spoke quietly. There was no response. "Dad?" she repeated, lifting her voice slightly.

Grandaddy stirred and turned his head a little in her direction, but not enough to look her directly in the face.

"Ev," he said. His breathing was labored

"Dad, Billy's here to see you."

"Billy?"

"Yes, Dad. Billy wants to say hello." She took me by the hand and pulled me toward the bed. He didn't open his eyes, but moved his hand toward the edge of the bed until it ran against the side of the plastic tent.

"Billy," he said, gasping for breath. "Billy, you'll be quiet, won't you? You won't make any noise will you?"

"Yessir."

"You'll be quiet, won't you, Billy?"

"Yessir."

"Come on now, Billy." My mother took me by the shoulders and pulled me away. Grandaddy turned his head back. He hadn't opened his eyes. He lay still, gasping, as my mother led me from the room.

My father milked late the next evening. The weather had turned cold, and he had wrapped the new pipe running down the outside of the milk house. "Funny," he said as he taped the strips of rock wool around the bare metal, "pipe never freezes up near the spring, although it can't be more than an inch or two underground. Only freezes at this end."

The milking barn was warm. My father and Dove moved silently from cow to cow, washing their udders, placing the suction cups on their teats, and carrying full five-gallon buckets of milk into the milk house where they strained it into ten-gallon cans. The cows stood quietly, eating a mixture of grain and silage which gave off a bittersweet smell of fermented corn. Some of them dozed when they finished, others stood chewing their cud, occasionally belching and rattling the stanchions with the heave. I imagined they liked the barn with its smells, the rhythmic pulsing of the valves on the De Laval milkers, and the steady drone of the milking machine motor.

With the milking finished, the equipment washed and placed on its racks, the three of us walked down the hill toward our house in the near darkness. My father carried a gallon bucket of milk still warm from the cows. The train rushing through Troutville sounded real close. We could hear the rapid pulse of its pistons beneath its whistle pattern, three long blasts, each beginning loudly, tapering off, then fading slowly away.

"Ray would say that's the 6:05 out of Staunton," my father said, speaking of Grandaddy. "It's nearly 6:15; he's running late." He stared into the dim gray distance toward the sound, then we continued on our way, no one saying anything about the number of lights up at Grandaddy and Nana's house and the number of cars out front, one of them a long gray Buick. But later that night I heard my mother crying in the kitchen, and the conversation went on softly for a long time.

"Doctor Davis isn't saying much," someone said.

Everything went still for a few moments; then I heard my mother tell my father that she wanted me to see Grandaddy one last time. I was in bed, but I hadn't been able to get to sleep. At her statement I suddenly felt hot.

I had only vague notions about death and the kinds of sickness that caused it. Grandaddy's sickness had taken all the joy out of my parents and the relatives who came to see us. The days dragged with a heavy grayness, and I didn't want to see him again. I scrunched way down under the covers and pulled them up over my head.

When my mother opened the bedroom door I closed my eyes and tried to modulate my breathing, hoping that if she saw me asleep she would go back to the kitchen and let me alone.

"Billy? Billy?" she whispered quietly, trying not to awaken my sister sleeping in her crib in the corner of the room.

"Billy?" she whispered again, but louder and shook me by the shoulder.

I opened my eyes halfway, still trying to look dazed. She knelt by the bed. "I want you to come up to Grandaddy's with me. Get up now, and let's go." She spoke quietly, but her voice was firm. The cold air hurt and made me shiver and feel small as I crawled out of the covers.

My grandparents lived in a four-room house with a screened porch across the front. You entered on wooden steps that gave with your weight in the summer, but seemed brittle and unyielding in the winter cold under a skiff of new snow. From the porch the main door to the house opened into a living room. The kitchen, where all the relatives sat drinking coffee around a table, lay straight ahead. The door to the right led to the bedroom where Grandaddy lay beneath the plastic canopy. Everyone was quiet as my mother and I walked through the door. Aunt Lillian, a registered nurse from Roanoke, stepped quickly from the kitchen, her finger raised to her lips for silence.

"Maybe you'd better not go in now," she said to my mother. "He's having a rough time."

Low sounds came from the darkened room. In a few minutes a man dressed in a dark suit with a stethoscope hanging from his neck appeared in the doorway. He paused briefly and rubbed his eyes with the tips of his fingers before coming into the dim light of the living room. My mother and Aunt Lillian went up to him. He shook his head and motioned them into the kitchen where they began to talk in subdued voices.

I crept to the bedroom door, but I didn't want to go in. I could see the plastic tent that hung above Grandaddy and the faint outline of his form beneath it. He didn't move, and the room was quiet. Then I heard his voice, softly, just above a whisper, as if he were singing a child to sleep: "Give me five minutes more, only five minutes more."

"Momma doesn't like living alone," my mother said one evening at the dinner table. "She's invited Granny to come and live with her."

"That's fine," my father replied, "but do the two of them need that house?" He meant the slightly larger, four-room house up on the hill, apparently feeling the squeeze of our small summer house as a year-round residence.

"Well, it's mother's house. After all she and Daddy put up most of the money for this place!"

My mother never forgot that part of Grandaddy's retirement money had made the down payment on the farm. It galled her that my father could so easily put aside the role my grandparents had played in purchasing his home.

He lived in a tension, desiring wealth and comfort, yet always fighting a shadow of deprivation. He hadn't suffered in the depression years. He'd worked at odd jobs, even hauled some bootleg whiskey through the mountains of western Virginia in a stripped-down Hudson. "I never seem to get ahead," he often lamented.

He looked sidelong at the role of gentleman farmer and began quoting James Whitcomb Riley, whom he'd read as a child. He liked Riley's Farm Rhymes, especially the lines,

"When the frost is on the pumpkin and the fodder's in the shock/ And you hear the kyouck and gobble of the struttin' turkey-cock." He sometimes delighted my sister and me by placing his hands on top of his head and causing his biceps and pectoral muscles to flex and quiver, seemingly of their own volition. He also kept an eight-iron handy. He'd take it into the pasture or side yard and practice chip shots, sometimes with a real ball; more often, he'd simply clip the heads off of dandelions or heft small lumps of cow manure into the air. Before every shot he'd look off into the distance and yell "fore," lopping off the word like a drill sergeant counting cadence, so the word actually came out "fooorp."

But now in his mid-forties he surpressed his strongest athletic urges or he worked them off in the fields and the milking barn. After ten years of marriage he lived on a farm that wasn't really his and in a house less than a third the size of the one he had grown up in. Then Great-grandmother came, another strand in an accretive web of gray, another reminder that he'd never win laurels or be chaired through a market place.

Lavender

Great-grandmother Whitescarver was in her nineties when she came to live on the farm with us in the spring of 1948. Like Nana she was a small woman, slightly stooped, but always neatly dressed, except when she unhooked her stockings from her corset and allowed them to bag around her ankles. She wore her white hair rolled back in a tight bun, and her thick, wire-rimmed glasses made her blue eyes look big.

Granny's calling my grandmother Laura seemed strange to me. The links between me and my mother and Nana seemed as clear and ordered as tines on a pitchfork; but Granny came from another age and place. My mother warned me so often to be careful around Granny that I began to suspect that if I ran into her she'd shatter into little pieces.

She and Nana slept in the same room in the four-poster double bed that Grandaddy had died in. The room also contained a bureau, a highboy, and a rocking chair with an antimacassar on its headrest. A small braided rug lay in the center of the floor. The room smelled of camphor and lavender and was as emotionally complicated as the delicate scrollwork on the back of Granny's silver hairbrush.

She once mistook for sass something I'd said to her and slapped me in the face so hard that I reeled backward into the kitchen table. Later, she came all the way to the milking barn to apologize. "I'm sorry," she said and took me by the hand. "Laura told me what you said. And

I shouldn't have acted so hastily. You know I'd never do anything to hurt you." Her voice quivered as she spoke and her lips looked blue. Her hands were slim and pale. Blue veins forked across the backs of them and down through swollen knuckles. I was surprised at how cold her hands felt against mine on such a warm evening, and even in the barn among odors of manure, ground feed, and heated bodies of cows, she leaned close and I could see the intricate web of lines etching her face and smell her lavender perfume.

Billy Wayne knew that stump water caused freckles but would prevent pimples if you bathed your face in it after a rain. He washed in stump water after every rain and his face was covered with freckles. Following his lead I risked freckles over the possibility of pimples and washed my face in the dirty brown liquid whenever possible. I later developed a full complement of pimples but never acquired a single freckle.

Stump Water

A small boy with thin arms, stickweed legs, wavy blond hair, and pale blue eyes, Billy Wayne Booth knew where to find the best grapevines for swinging and the easiest trees for climbing. He knew that tea brewed from sassafras roots in the spring would thin your blood and help you tolerate the summer heat. He knew when to pick ginseng and that its roots could be made into medicine. He called the knots from dead pine trees "lightwood" and knew that they were good for starting fires because they were rich in resin. Each spring Billy Wayne gathered morels in paper pokes, and by early summer he knew where to locate the fullest huckleberry patches along the crest of Tinker Mountain.

He cut evenly proportioned hickory forks to fashion gravel shooters, and he could carve whistles with tones as mellow as a flute's from yellow poplar branches. He crafted match stick shooters from spring-loaded clothes-pins and knew how to load wooden matches head first so they'd ignite and shoot away in flames when you pulled the trigger, or if you licked the match head before loading it, it would arch away in a long stream of blue smoke like a wounded plane. Billy Wayne could run along the side of a ridge at full speed without missing a step, and he knew how to hill up potatoes and milk the family cow, even though when he milked his pale hands trembled and a crow's foot of blue veins radiated back from his white knuckles.

He also believed that catamounts still roamed the mountains and often told me about how his father had been stalked by one along an old road skirting the lower hollows of Tinker between his home and mine. When I visited the Booths and stayed late, Billy Wayne often walked part of the way with me along that road. At the big rock where the stalking and near-attack allegedly took place, he'd grow wide-eyed and say, "I reckon I'd better get on home 'fore Poppa misses me." Then he'd fly back along the road, and leave me alone in the gathering dark.

He did that on a Saturday after I'd spent a day with him and two of his older brothers, Walter and J.E. We climbed the steep places in the mountains for a while, swung on wild grapevines, talked and played tag. After a lunch of brown beans and corn bread we rested in the shade of apple trees in the orchard behind the house. Suddenly, Man, a small dog Walter had carried home one day, began barking wildly at the mouth of a hole beneath one of the trees.

"It's a groundhog! I'll bet Man's treed a groundhog!" Walter said. He dropped to his knees and peered into the hole. We all gathered around him.

"Let's dig him out for dinner!" said Billy Wayne. He leaped to his feet and dusted the knees of the baggy gray dress pants he'd worn all week.

"Yeah, let's," J.E. echoed. "Poppa'd sure like that."

We began digging urgently, laboring with our hands, aided by several sticks. As we worked Man paced around us, lunging in to dig frantically every few minutes, shoving his nose far into the pit. His excitement kept us busy for nearly an hour.

"Wait a damn minute," Walter finally said, standing back. "We're beating ourselves to death. Billy Wayne, run down to the barn and bring a mattock and shovel."

"Yeah!" J.E. added, suddenly comprehending the ingenuity of Walter's suggestion. "Then we could really dig him out!"

Billy Wayne ran to the barn without a word and returned with the essential tools. Again we dug, each of us taking a turn with the mattock. Man growled and lunged repeatedly into the widening pit. With every attack we backed off, expecting he'd drag the groundhog out for the kill. We'd be blooded, justified, and rewarded with fresh meat.

We dug until we'd lost track of time and were disgusted with Man's energy. Walter finally tossed the mattock aside and stepped back from the hole. "Hell, I don't think that dog smells a damn thing."

"Man, you bastard!" J.E. dropped the shovel and shuffled away from the mound of earth and stood by Walter. "Maybe he don't smell nothin'!"

Billy Wayne crawled to one side. I squatted near him while Man continued to growl and lunge into the pit. His stiff tail waved back and forth like a curved spike.

"Come out of there, Man!" Walter shouted. He rushed at the little dog, grabbed him by the scruff of the neck, and flung him down the hill. Man yelped once or twice as he rolled, but quickly regained his legs and commenced a low-dog-slink back toward the tree. Walter stretched out on his back, keeping an eye on Man, who crept to within a few yards of where we were sitting, never taking his eyes off Walter and the pile of new earth.

Everything went quiet for a few minutes. A light wind rustled the new leaves and blossoms on the apple trees. A few green flies buzzed around the pit, a sure sign the den was occupied.

"We sure turned a lot of earth," Billy Wayne said.

"Yeah," said J.E. He glanced toward the tree just to be sure.

The wind died and we could hear honeybees working through the clover around us. Then there was a sound, a rustling, near the hole.

"Shit! Walter!" J.E. cried, suddenly scrambling away from the tree.

"What?" came the muffled response. Walter lay on his back, his arms folded over his eyes.

We turned just as a full-grown skunk stepped up on the mound of earth in front of the pit. He came quietly, even nonchalantly, like a man in a tuxedo stepping from a theater to have a smoke and test the evening air. For a second everyone was still and the skunk elevated his nose once or twice, sampling the environment.

But peace in nature is never permanent. Man spun out of his crouch with a growl and hit the skunk like a small brown thunderclap. Billy Wayne leaped to his feet just as the skunk let fly his first load of scent. Billy moaned low and choking as the spray wafted over his face and chest. He spit and flung himself, crab-like, half running and crawling, but mainly falling down the hill. Once out of range he began rubbing his face urgently with handfuls of grass and dirt, swearing violently.

I felt the first wave of stench roll over me and explode in my lungs. Gasping for breath I lunged away from the tree, trying to rake the smell off with my hands as I stumbled down the hill. At the bottom I threw myself on the grass, rolling and squirming to scrape away the terrible stench.

"Wait, Man! Goddam!" Walter screamed. He tried to stand up to avoid the spray, but tripped and rolled backward just behind Man, who by this time had the skunk firmly in his jaws, growling, shaking and waving him around like a plume. Walter groaned and sputtered out of the fray. At the bottom of the hill he stood with his arms out and dangling like a scarecrow, vowing he'd "kill that damned little son-of-a-bitch."

As the rest of us fled, J.E. leaped nimbly about like a barefoot dancer on hot pavement, waving his arms and yelling, "It's a skunk! It's a skunk!" He managed to scramble away relatively unscented, except for a dampness on the leg of his trousers.

Man tossed the skunk until it was thoroughly dead. He sneezed several times to purge the scent from his nose and dragged himself in the grass. Proud of his kill, he trotted up to each of us, seeking pats and congratulations for his prowess.

In a panic we ran to the spring at the bottom of the hill and waded in hoping to wash off more of the scent. "It won't do any good," Billy Wayne cautioned. "You have to bury clothes in loam for a month to get rid of the smell of skunk." But we rolled in the long grass anyway, then took our clothes off and washed them with sand and mud from the creek below the spring and waited, naked, chewing orchard grass and discussing the event while our clothes dried.

"I feel like I've been baptized with a rare ointment," Walter said.

"Yeah, me, too." J.E. lay back in the grass with a yawn.

Billy Wayne didn't even put his clothes back on to walk along the old road with me, and that's when he told me about the stump water. Right out of the blue as we passed by the big rock where his father had confronted the catamount, he said that stump water would keep off pimples. We had stopped near the big rock and Billy Wayne walked over to a rotting chestnut stump, and reached in with both hands as if he were dipping into a fountain and rubbed the water on his face.

"I sure stink. I smell like I've been dead for a week. Poppa'll have a fit."

"You going to bury your clothes?"

"Maybe. Poppa may kill me for messin' up my britches. You afraid of dying?"

"I never thought much about it."

"I do. I watched my Uncle John die. He was just standing in the kitchen and suddenly looked puzzled, then scared, and fell to the floor, and that was it."

"I'm sorry," I said, not sure how to respond to the instant seriousness of the conversation. From the adjacent ridge a whippoorwill commenced its repetitious call.

"It's getting late," Billy Wayne said, suddenly aware of how dark it was along the road. "See Ya," he whispered, almost under his breath and turned and raced down the tree-lined road as though down a tunnel, dodging tree limbs and rocks that had tumbled off the ridge. I watched his naked body become small and ghost-like in the shadows, and long after he'd disappeared in the darkness, I could hear his footsteps, never missing a beat.

Honey in the Comb

In the spring of 1952 raven-haired Melva Trent came from the seventh grade room to the top of the landing at the west end of Asbury Elementary and smiled down on the boys gathered at the foot of the steps.

"Let's see, Melva," one of the boys yelled.

"Yeah!" other voices agreed, and Melva approached the edge of the landing.

"What do you want to see?" she asked in a strange, deep voice. She smiled as if she knew a secret.

"You know!" the boys replied. "Let's see!"

Suddenly Melva flipped her skirt up far enough to reveal the secret whiteness of her thighs.

"Yeah!" the boys cheered. Melva turned and lifted the rear of her skirt briefly, then darted through the doorway.

"Melvaaah! Melvaaah! Melvaaah!" the boys yelled, and more gathered like bees around a fallen fruit.

Melva peeked through the doorway. "What?" she asked.

"Melvaaah!" the boys called again, all smiles. "Melvaaah!"

"No!" She giggled and ducked back into the building. The boys chanted her name until Melva again peered through the door. She rejected them, laughed and vanished. They called her back.

"I can't. Someone might tell Mrs. Henderson."

"No they won't, Melva. Let's see!"

Melva demurred, then spun around three times, flaring out her dress to reveal the full form of her legs and the contours of her white-clad bottom. A shiver of excitement buzzed through the thickening crowd. The boys in front cheered. Quieter ones in the rear smiled and elbowed one another. A few chewed their lips in pensive studies.

"Melvuuuh! Melvuuuh! Melvuuuh!" the crowd chanted in deeper tones.

"What's going on down there?" a voice called from one of the seventh grade windows. Melva darted back into the building and the boys scattered. Moments later Mrs. Henderson extended her arm through the raised window and shook her brass bell. Recess was over, and Melva missed school the next day. She returned and didn't smile for nearly a week and never teased the boys from the top of the steps again.

Asbury School stood on a hill above Cousin Laura and Cousin Ben Birch's house in Haymakertown, so close that the bees residing in Cousin Ben's hives spent the better part of each spring and fall sipping nectar from the urinals in the boys' outhouse.

Asbury was red brick with a long row of tall white windows along each side and topped by a slate roof. A row of gnarled cedar trees lined the front or south side, perfect for games of chase and tag.

Inside, the school was an accumulation of smells: lunch boxes and new books and old desks and sweaty children, perfumed teachers, newly oiled floors, and fresh shellac on the dark oak trim. In the spring of my first year someone flung a strawberry up to the molded metal ceiling, where it remained, a small black spot, for the next five years that I attended Asbury.

Four rooms housing seven grades comprised the academic heart of the school. Only the seventh grade had its own room. Grades one through six shared the other three large rooms, two grades in each. Teachers strolled from one side of the room to the other, parceling out work to separate grades and talents and widely ranging interests.

A small alcove at the west end of the building housed a library with shelves of books, among them a set of Zane Grey novels and at least one other book by Will James, a cowboy writer, who claimed that even in the forties a horseman could ride from the Canadian border to Mexico without crossing a fence if he picked his way carefully. From the window of the fourth and fifth grade room I watched the seasons change across a hill of broom sedge rising out of a hollow near Cousin Ben and Cousin Laura's house and wondered what lay beyond the blue haze of the mountains farther west. I also read a book about building steam engines and dreamed with Alfred Warrick about building a small one from a picture of a model.

For social functions the seventh grade room contained a raised stage, and the wall separating that room from the fifth and sixth grade room was a sliding door that opened up the entire south half of the building.

Bluegrass bands drew the largest crowds. The musicians wore western hats and played guitars, fiddles, banjos, "taterbug" mandolins, and at least one thumped a bass. They bowed, strummed and plucked with dead-pan faces, the lead singers closing their eyes to croon the choral parts of "Blue Moon of Kentucky Keep on Shinin'," or they'd cup their hands over their mouths to moan like a sad train whistle for "The Orange Blossom

Special," or two or three would lean toward each other and sing in high-pitched nasal harmony to emphasize the passion in "The Wild Wood Flower."

Country music had definite rhythms and stories about real people and places like Clifton Flowers who lived on Wolverton Mountain. The thump and slap of guitars, the clucking banjos, the thin wheeze of fiddles fascinated me, and I attempted to imitate their sounds with my voice.

In fourth grade I played Joseph to Nancy Walker's Mary in the Christmas program. We didn't speak. Nancy, with her round face, dark eyes, and black hair flowing from the edges of a pale blue scarf, smiled into the crib near a bale of straw at the foot of the stage. I stood behind her self-consciously, one hand behind my back, the other gripping a makeshift shepherd's staff, as kings in old bathrobes and high-topped work shoes with Cat's Paw rubber heels stomped onto the stage bearing gifts from a place called O-r-i-e-n T-a-r. They knelt solemnly before a doll in a wooden bushel apple box with Layman Brothers Orchards stencilled on it in blue letters while a group of second and third graders with runny noses sang "Silent Night."

Mothers wondered as children who split kindling, milked cows and slopped hogs in the evenings and mornings were momentarily transformed into figures at the heart of Christian mythology. I didn't smile the whole time, even when Steve Frantz, Billy Wayne Booth, D.R. Wood, and Peewee Harris giggled and made faces from the rear of the room.

Each room at Asbury was equipped with a pot-bellied stove for heat and a galvanized, two-gallon bucket, a single dipper, and a small tin basin for drinking and

60

washing. Some children avoided drinking from the communal dipper by bringing cups from home. Others turned the dipper at odd angles, seeking unused drinking points on the rim. Some children also balked at washing in the communal pan, but teachers insisted that everybody rinse hands in the bluish-gray water. Almost no one escaped the ritual.

First and second graders who bathed regularly at home were awarded small blue stickers representing bars of soap. These were placed on a chart by our names so we could keep track of who washed and who didn't each month. "Why, Billy, you got four bars of soap this time," Patsy Wright cooed one Monday morning, loud enough for everyone to hear, and Billy Wayne and D.R. mocked her praise and tone to me during recess all that day and most of the next. Some children took pride in rows of soap bars stretching beyond their names. Some accumulated only a few stickers, and others didn't wash or look at the chart at all.

Outhouses, one for the boys and one for the girls, sat on opposite sides of the hill below the school building with no running water or heat. They were four-holers contained in small buildings surrounded by high board fences for privacy. Although utilitarian and unpleasant, the boys' made a splendid fort for prolonged games of cowboys and Indians. In the heat of late spring and early fall, however, it tended to a ripeness tolerable to only the most stalwart of buckaroos. You had to be careful, too, of the honeybees gathering at the urinal trough. If your aim was accurate you could knock 'em down, but most of the time they managed to escape back to the hives down at Cousin Ben's.

So for nine months we daydreamed over our books between recesses and played marbles the whole school year. We slipped away from the school grounds to buy nickel cakes, taffy mint juleps and Mary Janes at Looney's store. And once in a corner of the school yard Manuel Grubs said that if I showed him mine he'd show me his, but I didn't. Mainly we prepared for adulthood. We fought, teased the girls, fell in love and out again, and tried to outdo each other in games of tag, cookiewitch, and baseball. But Curtis Meyers could outrun us all and climb a tree like a squirrel and swing like Tarzan from grapevines below the school yard on the Freeman place and find more beechnuts there than the rest of us. The girls gasped in amazement and called his name as he carried the small triplex seeds up to the fence, temporarily forgetting that a grinning Curtis, loaded with navy beans, often clambered aboard the morning bus and giggled as he passed a gas far surpassing that of common folk for potency and range. The more reserved among us boys were stunned and dismayed at the ease with which the girls turned their backs on us for handfuls of beechnuts.

On a soft, unassuming afternoon in late autumn of my sixth year at Asbury school, Billy Wayne, D.R., and I were playing in the driveway behind an early bus that had stopped to take on its complement of riders. I don't remember whether it was Billy Wayne or D.R. who decided to toss a handful of gravel into the exhaust pipe of the stopped bus so we could watch them spew out as the bus pulled away. At any rate, because we enjoyed an alliance, a special camaraderie, and called ourselves a gang, we assented to the deed with a spontaneity peculiar to children who seize upon opportunities for mischief with great ease and little thought. But our amusement went awry. Another child who had been watching from across the playground reported us to Mrs. Henderson, who sped to the scene.

She immediately asked who had tossed the stones into the tailpipe. I distinctly remember pointing to the culprit, but to my surprise, he pointed to the other boy, who by some wrinkled logic, pointed at me. Mrs. Henderson repeated the question, and we chanted the same warped response.

"No! Billy Wayne did it!"

"No, I didn't! D.R., he did it!"

"Billy did it! Billy threw them in!"

We shouted and stabbed our fingers in the air and stood red-faced, raging in separate, incoherent voices.

On our farm we raised hogs for a number of years. Hogs are basically unassuming creatures. They enjoy food and rest in abundance. If these are provided hogs are docile and generally goodhearted. But if you attempt to drive them into places that appear to them frightening or unsuitable hogs become mindless demons. Quiet grunts rise to squeals. The more you try to force them the more determined they become to resist. Snouts become crowbars. Squeals intensify to siren screams and stubby legs churn like pistons. For one brief moment in that dimming afternoon sun, my friends and I fled truth and reason with the blind fury of hogs fleeing the confines of a dark chute.

Mrs. Henderson questioned us a third time, her voice more tense and piercing. We returned the same clawing response. Seeing that she was not going to get to the heart of the matter and angry with us for forcing her to stricter measures, she spanked each of us with a long perforated paddle. I rode the school bus home that afternoon chafing under the sting of the paddle, but rankling even more at my helplessness before a storm of emotions beyond my understanding or control. Someday I would know; someday I would figure it all out.

At the end of that year I left Asbury. Near the close of school Cousin Laura Birch presented my mother with a quart of comb honey from the previous fall, thick, dark and sweet, but with a strange aftertaste, musky and sour like tea brewed from sweet gum and locust blossoms.

We'd come into the hollow one morning after milking and were sitting together on the side of a bank across the creek from a small hickory. He heard sounds that meant something to him, but not to me. We'd been sitting for a long time. I thought hunting would be lots of shooting with game falling like rain. I sat with my back against a stump and my legs stretched out. The barrel of my .22 rifle lay along my legs, the end of it resting between the toes of my shoes. Every now and then I'd draw a bead on a passing red ant and make a quiet sound of a gun going off — "Pooooosh." After each imaginary shot he'd lean toward me and say, "Be quiet, dammit."

In practice sessions he'd warned me to keep the muzzle of the gun up and the bolt forward, but not cocked, until I was ready to shoot. I guess the bolt got shoved all the way down accidentally while I was squirming around sighting at red ants. He moved suddenly like he'd seen something, cocked his Winchester and raised it to his shoulder. I also strained to detect any movement in the hickory and must have been tapping my finger on the trigger. The gun went off, "Bang!"

Small fragments of dirt spattered the leaves in front of us, and a long scar with a hole at the end of it appeared in the dirt just inches from my feet. The edges of the hickory tree he'd been watching shook violently as several squirrels leaped for safety. Their dark gray forms streaked along the branches of bordering trees and vanished into the foliage.

He was suddenly transformed from a sitting position to a standing one.

"Dammit, Boy. Don't you know you came within half an inch of blowing your toe off, maybe even your foot?"

"Yessir," I replied. In that instant I wished I'd never seen a rifle or ever wanted to go hunting.

We left the hollow with unloaded guns, he walking behind me as we made our way back to the barn. He never mentioned the incident and didn't take me hunting for over two years.

A Thin Line

By 1954 the bull pines in the pasture up near the mountain were taller than any man, and clusters of blackberry briers had sprouted along the dry creek bed running through the center of the pasture.

In the early fall of that year my father bought a light-weight J.C. Higgins 12-gauge, single-shot and gave it to me for squirrel hunting. He carried a model 97 Winchester, over four feet long with a visible hammer. The gun was old and heavy and handed down from my great-grandfather who had fought for the Confederacy. His initial, "G," for Gabriel, lay engraved on a small silver tab embedded in the butt of the pistol grip on the stock.

In all our hunting together my father did relatively little shooting and almost never missed. On quail hunts, when the dogs made a stand, he'd often wave me forward so I could make the first shot on the covey ride. Hunting rabbits, he'd point out likely thickets, and if a rabbit jumped, he'd step aside, allowing me to shoot first. More than once after I'd blazed away ineptly with both barrels of the 16-gauge double he'd given me for jump shooting, he'd throw his shotgun to his shoulder, make the lethal shot, and say, "I just blacked your eye," then wink.

He loved to hunt, but as he grew older he was less interested in killing animals and preferred grouse hunting since more time was spent hunting than shooting. Besides, grouse hunting was a form of communion and took place in the secret places on the south side of Tinker Mountain.

So when we squirrel hunted together, he must have seen as many squirrels as I did. On our way back down the mountain, he'd often tell me about watching squirrels play chase, and once he described how a chipmunk had sniffed up to him and rested a paw against his shoe.

"Hey, Boy! Hey!" his voice called through the near dark, ruffling my dreams. The pressure of his hand on my shoulder pulled at me. "Let's go!"

The linoleum floor was cold, so I dressed quickly and crossed the hallway to the kitchen where he stood at the sink preparing his favorite quick breakfast, two raw eggs beaten into a glass of milk.

"Here's to good bowels," he said, lifting the glass as if in a toast. I could never eat breakfast that early in the morning.

"You'll learn," he said, placing the empty glass in the sink. "You ready? It's time; they'll be cutting in another twenty minutes." He picked up his faded hunting coat and Winchester shotgun and started out the front door.

The grass was wet and cold, and a light fog hung in the dark hollow up from the barn. My shoes got soaked and the legs of my jeans were wet to the knees as we climbed the slippery path into the mountain. The woods were still dark and damp, and hermit thrushes produced croaking sounds as they flitted through the low branches near the edge of the tree line.

I eased down the ridge to a stump twenty yards from a tall hickory. False dawn brightened the top of the ridge where I'd left my father. I waited, listening to the heavy dew drip from leaves. An hour passed with no sign of a squirrel. A rooster crowed over at the Custer place nearly a mile away. I began to suspect that the hickory had been cut out. Then, behind me, a branch end dipped and sprang back as a squirrel leaped from it to the branch of a nearby tree. I didn't turn right away. A sudden movement might spook the squirrel. Custer's rooster crowed again, a small far-away call, and a mosquito began singing around my ears. I waited, listening for the rustle of leaves or the clicking of small claws against tree bark. The mosquito whined closer until it lit somewhere behind my right ear. I raised my hand and passed it slowly by my head. The small whine began again then stopped. A breeze rustled through a grove of maple saplings near the tree line fifty yards down the ridge.

It shifted slowly up the mountain and struck the upper branches of the trees around me, and in its wake the squirrel streaked along a high branch to the near side of an oak. It hung for a moment, gathering for a leap. I saw it move and threw the shotgun to my shoulder, cocking it as it came up, then squeezing the trigger just as the squirrel sprang for the hickory. Twigs and broken branches rained down and a few leaves spun in the air as the blast echoed through the mountain and died away. The squirrel thrashed for a moment, regained its grip, then raced from the tangled branches toward the heart of the tree. My hands were shaking; I'd shot too soon.

The empty shell popped into the leaves, still smoking as I broke the gun open, quickly slipped a new shell into the chamber, and clicked the gun shut. The squirrel might try to run. I'd be ready this time.

The mountain was suddenly quiet. I raised my hand slowly and pressed my fingers against the stinging sensation on the back of my neck and pulled away the remains of a bloated mosquito.

In the valley below someone started the engine of a baler, probably Henderson's Dearborn. The engine popped and revved quickly to full speed, the sound low but clear. In a few moments it commenced a rhythmic surging as the horse head rose and fell, packing the hay into bales.

I was surprised at how late it had gotten, almost ten-thirty. Another mosquito appeared and buzzed around my head. My neck ached as I strained to detect the squirrel among the dark leaves and glaring patches of sunlight. Traffic increased along 779. The swish of tires echoed off the mountain and Henderson's baler pulsed in the distance.

A small rustling of leaves came from high in the upper branches, then a crashing sound as the squirrel suddenly fell through the tree and flattened against a low limb not more than twenty yards from where I stood — too close for a good shot, but the sound startled me. I threw my shotgun to my shoulder and aimed. The squirrel didn't move. I hesitated, lowering the gun, thinking maybe he'd seen me and had frozen against the limb as they often did when cornered. Higher up on the ridge a nut dropped from a scale bark hickory and thunked against a hollow log. Several birds swept into a pin oak nearby and rained down debris.

The squirrel remained locked against the branch. Taking advantage of the commotion and keeping the gun cocked and ready, I attempted to ease away from the tree to get a better shot. But the birds flew off as suddenly as they had appeared, and the mountain went still except for the baler throbbing in the distance and another mosquito singing around my ears. I stepped back, my foot riding down against a dead branch. It popped and the squirrel flinched but didn't run. A thin ribbon of red appeared along its throat and crept down the side of the limb.

"Make every shot count," my father insisted. He was particular about shooting: "One shot ought to be enough," he'd say. "A responsible hunter uses a shotgun properly so he doesn't tear up the game or cause unnecessary suffering." He told stories about a man he knew who often wounded squirrels and chased them through the woods with a club. "That's no way to hunt," he'd say with deep scorn in his voice. He often told about my grandfather hunting a whole season and never missing a shot, and about himself, hunting grouse and quail and making forty-five consecutive kills, then missing a rabbit running straight away from him — "Stupid; just plain stupid."

The squirrel started as if about to run, but remained in place, staring straight out along the limb. I raised the shotgun, then lowered it again, releasing the hammer, still too close for a good shot. The squirrel seemed unaware of the movement. Its eyes remained fixed on some point beyond the tree; its sides pulsed rapidly. A drop of blood pecked into the leaves below. I raised the gun again, determined to finish the squirrel; then, from across the ridge, a blast from my father's Winchester rolled through the mountain like waves of thunder. I heard the faint clatter as he pumped another shell into the chamber, and everything went silent again.

I lowered my gun and eased back several steps. The squirrel began to quiver and the tempo of its breathing increased.

"Were the soldiers brave?" I once asked Dove.

"Depends," he said after a long pause. "There's only a thin line between bravery and cowardice."

"Were you scared?"

"Yeah, everybody was scared. Some were so scared they ran, and some just shit their pants and stayed. You couldn't always tell which man you wanted to be. Combat is more about survival than duty and honor. Think about hunting if the squirrels could shoot back." Now that I thought about it, Dove never liked hunting or shooting guns.

The squirrel attempted to move again, but slipped on the limb. Another drop of blood fell into a small puddle collecting on a dead leaf, and the squirrel slumped precariously sideways.

Once on the slope near the milking barn my cousin Jim and I watched a kitten chasing small yellow butterflies hovering around some cow manure.

"Cats always land on their feet when they fall," Jim observed and picked the kitten up and let it drop. "See?" he said as it landed gingerly on its feet.

"Yeah, I know."

"Watch this!" He pitched the kitten higher. It landed on its feet again but much harder and tried to dart away. Jim grabbed it once more a hurled it much higher. It landed on its feet again, but lay still. A small drop of blood bubbled from its nose.

"Don't do that anymore, damn you!" I screamed at him.

"That's pretty great, don't you think?" he said, grinning maliciously. "It landed on its feet. Besides, cats have nine lives."

I felt helpless against his size and city-bred indifference. He didn't distinguish between inanimate objects and living things. The squirrel began to tremble, and I couldn't remember what had happened to the kitten, only the moment of cruelty and my own helplessness.

My father coughed on the far side of the ridge, and I thought I heard his footsteps in the leaves. Soon he'd call from the top of the ridge. The mountain was silent, no wind, not even the sounds of squirrels cutting in the distance. The rooster crowed again from the Custer place, but weaker this time, as if he were giving up for the day.

Moving back several steps I cocked the shotgun, then remembered that my father would hear the shot and surely ask how many squirrels I'd killed. I hesitated, lowering the gun and releasing the hammer. The squirrel coughed, his tail dropped over the limb. I raised the gun slowly but didn't cock it — a second shot for one squirrel. "Why were your shots so far apart?" my father might ask. "Did you miss the first time?"

The squirrel coughed again and shook, blood oozing from its mouth. My father whistled from the ridge top. My hands were shaking as I pulled the hammer back to the cocked position and aimed.

"Billy!" my father called. He was a hundred yards away, but his voice seemed closer.

I lowered the gun for a moment, then raised it again to shoot. But just before I pulled the trigger, the squirrel let go of the limb, struck the ground hard and rolled down the ridge, sprawling dead against a fallen limb a few yards from my feet.

"You do any good?" my father asked as I climbed to the top of the ridge.

"One," I replied, but didn't look at him.

"Just one? You usually do better than that." He jacked the shells out of his Winchester and dropped them into the pocket of his hunting coat. "What's wrong?" he asked, staring at me.

"Nothin'. How many did you get?" I asked. He threw the gun across his shoulder and moved down toward the edge of the woods.

"None."

"You shot once!"

"I'd heard one in a hickory over by the big rock — cuttings falling like rain. I must have worked around that tree for an hour, then I thought I saw him peeking out at me. Turned out to be a damned knot." He looked back and smiled but didn't stop or say anything more.

From the hill at the edge of the woods we could see up the valley, fields and patches of trees finally receding into light blue haze. Across the way Henderson had finished baling. His John Deere tractor and the red Dearborn baler stood outside the field dotted with small bundles lying prone in the high morning sun. A small figure of a man was closing the gate. We dropped below the tree line into the hot dry day of long grass and bull pines, all features of the landscape now sharply defined and brittle.

PART TWO

"Throw it away. Throw it away. Throw it away, now, boys," the foreman called again, and I could hear the faint clank of a rail against the metal plates as the men placed it on the ties. I listened to the calls and watched the gandy dancers until late in the afternoon. Beyond them I could see the pine tree at the end of our lane and the small patch of white beneath it.

An Uncertain Field

At first, I imagined a scrap of newspaper had blown against a pine tree near the end of our lane during a storm the night before. I looked again; an old man dressed in a wrinkled shirt, baggy brown trousers, and a battered felt hat sat motionless against the tree. A long stem of foxtail grass hung from his lips like an artist's paint brush poised in mid-stroke. The late-morning sun glinted on his gold wire glasses as he looked up with a bright, startled expression, like a deer suddenly glancing up from the far side of a field of tall grass.

"What say?" he murmured as I approached him. "Been ridin'?"

"Yeah," I replied, halting my bike in the gravel a few feet away.

"Where do you ride?"

"I've been up to Meyer's Store."

"How far?"

"About a mile. What're you doin'?"

"I'm here to show the trucks where to turn." He nodded toward the crew of men a few hundred yards behind him, laying track for a railroad through the middle of our farm. "Have to be here to tell the drivers where to dump the gravel."

The Norfolk and Western spur line from Cloverdale to the cement plant being built three miles west of our place had been under construction for several months along a railroad bed that had been surveyed and graded in the early thirties by men with teams of mules and slip-scrapers.

Now, over twenty years later, workmen had returned. In previous weeks they had labored through the Wright place, the Lackey place, the Potter place. They had cut into the east side of our farm, pushing down trees and building up the bed with heavy graders, earth movers and rollers. Dump trucks from the quarry in Blue Ridge spread gravel in an even ribbon over the smoothly scraped and packed earth. A section gang worked closely behind, laying a row of cross-ties and rails.

The old man suddenly turned toward the sounds of the workmen. "Gandy dancers. Hard work," he said softly. The foxtail grass bobbed in his lips.

"*Ready, boys. Ready, now,*" a foreman in a white pith helmet called in a lilting voice, and the gandy dancers moved to the rail pile near the end of the new track. "*Bow down. Bow down. Bow down, now, boys,*" he sang again, and the men bent to pick up a rail, six on each side. "*Heave, boys. Heave, boys. Heave, boys, now,*" and in a single quick movement the men lifted the rail with tongs. "*Come on down. Come on down. Come on down, now, boys,*" he began to wail in a cadence as he walked toward the end of the track. The men followed mechanically like a giant centipede. He sang again and they lined the rail up with the one preceding it. At a final call — "*Throw it away. Throw it away. Throw it away, now, boys,*" — the men lowered the rail onto a series of metal plates resting on wooden ties. Other men hammered in the anchoring spikes with long, sweeping strokes.

I'd watched the work crew toiling steadily toward our farm, fascinated by the rhythm of their movements, the foreman's steady cadence, and the pounding of the hammers. Some farmers in the neighborhood had tried to stop the railroad and the cement plant, afraid that dust from its smokestacks would spread over the valley. "But you can't stop progress," my father had argued, and the track crept relentlessly forward. The gandy dancers were dark brown from the sun and their backs and arms glistened with sweat.

The old man studied their regimented movements, now and then lifting his sunken eyes toward the massive rock jutting from the crest of Tinker Mountain. He seemed fascinated by the rock and the smooth glide of buzzards circling lazily in the air currents rising up its limestone cliffs.

"Where do you live?" he asked after a few moments, turning to face me. He sat with his back rigidly against the tree, his legs drawn up, his arms on his knees, and his slender hands dangling in front of his bony shins.

"There." I pointed up the lane past the railroad bed. I could see the top of our house above a row of sour cherry trees between the driveway and our front yard.

"I've been here since eight o'clock," he said, apparently not hearing my response to his question. "It's going on twelve now. Where'd you say you lived?"

"Up there. That's the top of our house sticking up above those trees."

"Yer Momma fix you lunch?"

"Yeah, when it's lunch time."

"That's nice. My landlady fixes mine, but she doesn't furnish me with much." He reached behind him to the other side of the tree, pulled out a brown paper bag, and slowly opened it with his skinny fingers.

Reaching into the bag he drew out what at first appeared to be little more than two lumps of waxed paper.

Carefully folding the empty bag and placing it in the grass beside him, he unwrapped the waxed paper and removed a small stack of saltine crackers and a small, rectangular block of cheese. I imagined his landlady, an older woman in a faded blue or pink house coat and worn cotton slippers, stuffing crackers and cheese grudgingly into a brown paper bag.

The old man leaned back against the tree and bit into a cracker. He was pale and gaunt. "I could bring you a sandwich," I said, easing my bike back into the lane. My mother made lunch precisely at noon, and I knew she'd be expecting me. "It wouldn't be any trouble."

"*Throw it away. Throw it away. Throw it away, now, boys,*" the foreman in the pith helmet sang.

"No, I guess not. I'll eat what I got." He glanced once more toward the section gang.

"My mom would fix it for you, or I could make it."

He continued watching as the drivers swung their hammers to set the spikes and the men handling the rails laid aside their tongs and gathered for lunch in the shade of a flatcar.

"Nope, I'd rather stay here. Can't take time to eat much."

My bike tires crunched the gravel in the road and spit small stones right and left as I cut back and forth across the center ridge in the lane. I thought again about carrying a sandwich to the old man and wondered if my mother would agree. It might seem impractical to her. She had strong opinions about what was useful and what wasn't. "You look only in one direction at a time," my father often teased her. "Don't be so twenty-four-hour-a-day practical. Dream a little!"

I halted my bike over a culvert beneath the lane, half-way between the tree where the old man kept his watch and the gandy dancers eating lunch beneath the flatcar. Water poured swiftly through the culvert because of heavy rains the night before, and a sheet of newspaper lay snagged on a rock several feet from the entrance. The portion clinging to the rock had already yellowed. The rest, like tattered white cloth, waved restlessly in the current.

"What old man? I haven't noticed any old man." My mother paused from rolling a pie crust and laid the rolling pin aside.

"He's by the pine tree," I replied. "I just saw him. He's there now. I want to take a sandwich to him."

"But if you take food to him you'd have to take it to all of the men. How long has he been there?"

"Since eight o'clock, he said. And Mom, he's hungry. One sandwich wouldn't hurt. Besides, he's not like the other men, and he's not with them." She picked up the rolling pin and passed it rapidly back and forth across the dough in different angles to make the crust thin and even.

"That's funny, I didn't see him when I went out to Ikenberry's." She laid the rolling pin down and walked to the front door, wiping her hands on her apron. From the doorway she glanced absently down the road, perhaps more to collect her thoughts than to see anything, since the row of cherry trees blocked her view. She'd picked earlier that morning, complaining that she couldn't reach the brightest, fullest cherries at the top of the trees. "I've got to get out there tomorrow," she said.

"More have ripened since this morning. I just hate to see them waste." Returning to her pie crust, she commenced rolling again, bearing down hard on the pin. Newly picked cherries sat in pans on the counter.

"Mom?"

"Doesn't he have a lunch?" she asked, wiping her forehead with the back of her hand. Wide streaks of gray sweeping back through her hair made her look severe.

"Yeah, but it's only soda crackers and cheese."

"Did he ask you to bring him a sandwich?"

"No, Ma'am, but he's hungry! I know he is!"

"Well," she began, her voice suddenly quieting the way it always did when she'd made up her mind, "I just don't think it's necessary for us to make a sandwich for some strange man who already has food. Besides, lunch is over." She quickly whisked the empty sandwich plate and milk glass from the table. "Now you go along and do your chores."

"But, Mom!"

"No! You have things to do. Have you finished your work at the barn? Did you wash up the milkers this morning?"

"No, Ma'am."

"Then go along, right now." She motioned me toward the front door and turned back to her pie crust.

"*Heave, boys. Heave, boys, now,*" the foreman's distant voice pulsed in the breezes playing through the open window of the milk house. From behind the deep sink and the soapy solution that stung my hands I listened to the repeated chants and pounding hammers and could see men moving back and forth along the railroad bed.

*"Come on down. Come on down. Come on down, now,
boys,"* the foreman's call sounded again and again
through the waves of afternoon heat radiating from the
tar paper roof of my uncle's house just below the milk
barn. The previous summer, before he had moved there
with his family, relatives had come for a visit, and I had
slept in a small room at the back of the house and stayed
in bed one morning past milking time, day-dreaming of a
young woman with long blonde hair and dark eyes. Her
name was Ruth, and we sat together under the weeping
willow tree by the spring. She leaned against me, speaking in a voice full of promise.

"Are you feeling all right?" my mother asked, her voice
jagged and loud. She stood in the doorway, eyeing me
suspiciously.

"Yes, Ma'am."

"What have you been doing?"

"Nothin'."

"Then you might just as well get up right now." Her
voice was hard like an ice pick stabbing into new ice.
*"You get up and get dressed. Twelve-year-old boys who day-
dream too much can get themselves into serious trouble."*
Without waiting for a reply she turned and walked away.
The screen door banged shut and I could hear her footsteps fading along the pathway leading away from the
front of the house.

The section gang worked through our farm for
several days. I don't remember precisely when they
finished. One morning after a heavy rain I rode my bike
to the new track and looked up and down the rails and

realized that our farm would always be in two parts: "You can't stop progress," my father insisted. All evidence of the men had washed away; all their footprints in the dust beside the track had vanished. The newspaper clinging to the rock near the culvert had disappeared, too. After so much activity our farm lay quiet, except for the chirring of the first few cicadas of the season. Even the matted-down foxtail grass where the old man had waited was beginning to stand back up. I didn't see him again and never discovered his name. But I remembered his eyes, soft and staring in the morning light, but nervous, too, like a deer watching strange forms waver and grow larger on the far side of an uncertain field.

In his middle years, my father took to sunbathing in the nude. He'd take a folding chair up into the pasture behind the barn and sit among the pine trees, now ten to fifteen feet high, or he'd go up to the far end of the hollow near the spring and sit along the edge of a grove of virgin hickories; and sometimes he'd sit in an open space on the hill above the house. In my rambles over the farm I'd often find the chair, but the first few times I discovered it I didn't know why it was there or why it was never in the same place, until one Sunday afternoon I stumbled on him in the feed lot behind the barn, sitting by the salt lick, naked except for sunglasses and a sock sheathing his penis. He looked startled for a moment then told me to get the hell on back home.

Aunt Mary

Aunt Mary and Uncle Roger came to live in the little house below the milk barn in 1953, where Aunt Mary spent the next four of her blonde summers in halter tops and form-hugging shorts. In her twenties then, she raced back and forth between the two houses, leaping the small creek that ran between them, on long, well-formed, evenly tanned legs coated with a finely textured down.

She wore her hair short and used make-up only once in a while, and when she laughed light danced in her blue eyes. She loved to joke and kept up a running banter with my father and was almost never ill. She seemed vulnerable and far away, seeking yet resistant.

"You're in love with her, and don't tell me you're not," my mother once remonstrated with my father in subdued tones when she supposed I couldn't hear. I heard the tension in her voice from across the yard. My father didn't reply, but I knew why the 40-power telescope lay in its sheath on a ledge in the milking barn above the little house.

Life seemed many-sided and haunted by moods that appeared and passed away as easily as summer storms. Uncle Roger worked in Roanoke at various jobs, selling for a while, then in the parts department of the Chevrolet dealership, then back to selling, vacuum sweepers or pots and pans or life insurance. Often he came home late or had to be gone overnight.

"Could Billy come down and stay with me?" Aunt Mary asked one evening when Uncle Roger was away.

She stood in the kitchen doorway as she spoke, and my mother raised her eyes from her sewing machine in the far corner of the room.

"Stay the night?" She repeated the key words of the question slowly as if she were tasting them.

"Well, yes. I sometimes get a little afraid. He could sleep on the sofa."

"The whole night?" My mother's voice dropped a full tone on the last word. "I don't know what a fourteen-year-old could do if there were trouble."

"I would just like to have someone in the house," Aunt Mary replied. Although her voice was calm she kept running her hands along the door frame as if inspecting cracks in the white paint.

"Bill!" my mother called to my father who was watching "Rawhide," his favorite TV show, in the living room.

"Bill! What do you think?"

"*Rollin', rollin', rollin',*" Frankie Laine's voice rang out, signaling the end of the show.

"About what?"

"About Billy staying down with Mary tonight?"

"*Keep them doggies rollin', Rawhide.*"

"I don't care," my father called above the theme.

"Well," my mother began hesitantly, but paused to rip a weak stitch out of the hem of her new dress. "I suppose it might be all right for tonight." She finished the sentence, frowning, and I couldn't tell at that moment whether she were upset at the ruined stitch or at Aunt Mary's request.

"Thank you," Aunt Mary replied. She motioned for me to get my things. I ran to my room and gathered up my toothbrush and feather pillow. We left quickly and I followed her down the hill and across the creek, which she leaped gracefully in the moonlight.

In the living room of the small house we sat on the sofa and Aunt Mary stretched her legs out to the coffee table as we watched TV. Light from the screen silvered the down on her upper thighs. I watched the TV, but kept glancing sideways toward Aunt Mary's legs, full and soft-looking from the edge of her red shorts to the straps of her sandals. Now and then she'd run her hands along her inner thighs, then reach down to her ankles and pull her hands upward over the calves of her legs.

I recalled Melva Trent, twirling at the top of the steps at school to show off her legs and panties and recalled, too, an earlier time when Aunt Mary and I had gone to a movie in Roanoke, just the two of us. It had rained while we were in the theater and when we came out our shoes squeegeed on the wet pavement.

"That's a strange sound, isn't it?" Aunt Mary asked, and I agreed. "It sounds like something else, though," she added, "and it's more fun." She just threw the line out; it struck once like a ball hurled from the top of a nearby building and passed into the night. She didn't pursue it, and we continued along the dark street in the mist and smell of new rain shining on the pavement.

At a station break Aunt Mary rose from the sofa and went to the kitchen a few steps away.

"Want half an apple?" she asked, as she opened the refrigerator. She pulled out a red fruit and polished it briefly against her shorts, then cut it in half. Returning to the sofa she sat closer to me and held out the larger half. She stretched her legs out again, near enough that they touched mine.

"Winesap. They're so good," she said and bit into her half, a large, wet bite. The juice from it spattered against my bare arm.

Just as the program resumed, a loud knocking came from the door, and Aunt Mary went to answer it. Before she reached the hallway, however, my mother burst into the room.

"Evelyn!" Aunt Mary exclaimed. "What's wrong?"

"I just think this is not a good idea," my mother stated, matter-of-factly. She gathered up my pillow from the end of the couch and stood back. "Let's go, Billy."

"Oh, Ev!" Aunt Mary walked over to the couch and stood with her arms at her side. "We're all right," she said, her voice low and determined.

"I know, but I think Billy should come back to the house with me."

Aunt Mary tried, but my mother wouldn't hear of any different arrangement and refused to explain her actions. The night didn't sit right with her, and she aimed to change the conditions. Aunt Mary stood in the doorway, watching as we crossed the creek, our feet thumping on the wooden bridge, and climbed the hill to the other house.

The summers passed and I found my father's sunning chair in odd places, often among the pines, sometimes on the hill above the main house, and occasionally at the head of the hollow near the mountain. His telescope remained in the milking barn, most of the time in its sheath, but now and again I discovered it standing unsheathed and upright on the ledge near the window overlooking the little house.

Aunt Mary, her long legs flashing in the sun as she hung out clothes or leaped across the creek on her way to the other house, never invited me to stay the night again, but when we played leap-frog in the pool or swam close to one another, the prickly sensation of her legs against my back or against my outer thigh stirred desires and vague regrets.

During those summer months, between canning and house cleaning, my mother spent long hours in the easy chair in my father's bedroom while he was at work, reading her Bible and another book she'd borrowed from a neighbor, *Science and Health, with Key to the Scriptures*, bound in blue leather. In the center of its front cover the smaller volume carried an emblem, a crown suspended halfway up the shaft of a tilted cross, embossed in gold.

The Pool

Each spring frogs gathered at the pool to copulate in long, sleepy-eyed embraces and lay their eggs in extended strands of a jelly-like substance with black dots. By late June a black tide of tadpoles lined the shallows, dispersing as swimmers moved into the water and gathering again as they passed. At night frogs chanted staccato choruses in the cool mountain air.

The summer of 1956 was dry. The pasture faded to a pale green with brown splotches. The creek behind the barnyard dried up, the one furnishing the pool slowed to a trickle, and so much water seeped away we quit swimming. My father finally opened the fence and allowed the cows to use the pool as a watering hole.

That winter cracks appeared in the thin concrete bottom. My cousins and I skated on the small patch of ice near the dam. Loose flakes of masonry crunched under our feet as we walked across the empty stretch of the pool near the shallow end.

The following spring my father once again took his hand level and made sightings along the creek that ran between the two houses. The pool could be kept full, he decided, if the water supply could be increased. He'd purchased a small tractor by then, so he wrapped one end of a log chain around the drawbar of the tractor and fastened the other end to the top hole in the beam of a horse-drawn bottom plow to make it run deep. While Uncle Roger drove the tractor, my father guided the plow to open the ditch for new three-inch terra-cotta pipe to be laid from a small dirt dam in the creek to the pool.

That summer we swam again, and the relatives came and picnicked each Sunday afternoon. At night my father built a fire in the barbecue pit and my mother and her brothers and sisters snapped their fingers through "Down by the River-side," and clowned, making faces and strange sounds as they sang "Nothin' Could be Fina' Than to be in Carolina in the Mawnin'." They held hands and swayed slowly back and forth as they harmonized through "Down by the Old Mill Stream" and "Shine on Harvest Moon." Sometimes one of them would forget the words or lose his place and begin to stutter or howl like a dog baying at the moon. They also liked to sing "Carry Me Back to Ol' Virginny," but only toward the end of the evening when they were tired and ready to quit.

Sometimes, when they sang an old, slow song, their voices flowed together in the midst of it like streams merging over a deep place. They leaned close together. Some closed their eyes. Others looked far into the night. They breathed in and expelled words in long, rhythmic cadences or until their song ended. Then they'd sit for a moment or two before giggling, embarrassed at having been drawn so far into their own harmony.

Often, when the relatives left, my father took a final swim. He'd sit on the dam and listen to the frogs tuning up for the night, first one, then another and another until their croaking blended to a harmonic chirring as loud as a cicada up close to your ear.

But the rains continued to fail and the pool lost water. By midsummer we stopped swimming, and during the following winter the bottom decayed more, leaving the concrete in small crumbling shards across the shallow half.

But my father delighted in the pool. It was for him a mark of distinction — with a swimming pool in the middle of the farm, even though we farmed mainly with a team of mules, we could hardly be called poor. The idea suited my father's temperament with all its complexities. He could never keep his priorities in order, and each year as the garden turned to weeds and the scrub pines in the pasture near the mountain extended fingers of new growth and spread their seed cones deeper into the heart of the field, we spent hours digging new trenches to pipe more water to the pool.

Yearly our efforts to use the pool became more frantic, until my father decided to put in a new bottom. He couldn't afford the cost of concrete, so he decided to pave it with asphalt. He purchased a fifty-five gallon drum of tar and had several tons of small gravel hauled from the quarry in Blue Ridge. His plan was simple. He would spread a layer of gravel in the bottom of the pool, pour hot tar over it, then spread a second layer of gravel over that. The layers could be easily packed with a lawn roller.

Heating the tar was a problem. Fifty-five gallon drums of tar are at least bulky, almost impossible to lift, much less to heat evenly to the appropriate temperature. My father decided to cradle the drum on its side in the arms of the barbecue pit and kindle a wood fire beneath it. To allow for the expanding tar he cut a hole in the top of the drum with an axe.

My uncles, aunts and cousins came from Roanoke to help with the task. We picnicked early in the afternoon. My mother cooked hamburgers on the barbecue pit so the fire would be ready when the men hoisted the drum into its arms. We laughed and joked and allowed that it would be nice to have the pool full again.

The workers completed their late lunch and prepared for the job, to be finished in the evening cool. Some spread the first layer of gravel while others gathered to watch the fire. They sang "Camp Town Races" and "There'll Be a Hot Time in the Old Town Tonight." They spoke in Uncle Remus dialect and told the story of "The Tar Baby." Buckets for carrying hot tar to the pool were placed near the spigot on the end of the drum. My father added more wood to the fire and we waited. Minutes passed, creaking into hours, but the tar wouldn't flow from the spigot. The buckets remained empty and uncles and aunts rested their elbows on the picnic table. Cousins darted back and forth across the first layer of gravel. The hiss of their speeding footsteps echoed off the pool wall.

My father added more wood, then more wood, until the flames leaped up the sides of the drum. "That ought to do the trick," he said.

"Bill," my mother questioned, "don't you think that might be too hot?"

"No," my father replied, and added more wood.

In a short while the first bubbles began to appear in the tar near the opening in the top. At first they humped up slowly and burst reluctantly. Relatives gathered around the pit, watching as the flames leaped along the sides of the drum.

"Nectar from the primitive earth," my father said, as he watched the deliberate progress of the bubbles. "Think how long that stuff was buried before someone pumped it out of the ground and barreled it for use — all that pressure."

Uncle Roger sounded the first alarm. "Oh, Lordy!" he said, "Bill, look at that!"

"What?" My father set his half-full cup of coffee on a nearby bench and stepped to his side of the drum.

"There!" Roger pointed to the hole in the top of the drum. A finger of expanding tar oozed over the sides of the opening and crept perilously near the leaping flames.

"What is it?" My mother rushed to the scene. Ever on the lookout for catastrophe, she quickly surmised imminent danger and flew into a panic. "Oh, do something!" she screamed at my father who was standing with a pained expression on his face.

The first blob of tar fell into the fire, creating a small explosion. The flames leaped further up the sides of the drum, igniting more of the black ooze. Within seconds the drum and barbecue pit were engulfed in flames rising far into the air. Sparks of burning tar flew in all directions, and my mother darted through the yard, rounding up children and calling to my father. "Bill! Do something! Call the fire department! The house! The house!" Twice she ran into the house and darted out again, apparently looking for the phone, which was in fact two hundred yards farther up the hill at the other house.

Uncles and aunts charged around gathering buckets and hoses to control the dancing blaze. Uncle David dragged a hose from the other side of the house and flopped it on the ground, then disappeared around the house leaving the hose to discharge water into the grass.

During most of the excitement, my father simply stood his ground. "Pretty, isn't it," he finally said to Aunt Mary standing next to him. By that point he'd probably realized that there was nothing anyone could do to put out the blaze. He gave up, satisfied to watch the fireworks. The flames rose higher as the tar began to boil in the drum and spill over more rapidly. The house was never really threatened and gradually all the relatives' panic subsided and they also gathered to watch the spectacle. Cars stopped along Route 779, too, and for a moment our farm was the center of attention. No one called the fire department.

The next day I went down to the pool. My father was already there. His work shoes made crunching sounds in the burned grass around the barbecue pit. "A mess, isn't it?" he said, kicking the cracked and blackened stones. He ran his hand over the hard globs of tar that had fallen on the picnic table and the benches, then walked down to the edge of the pool and stood on an outcropping of shale. Specks of tar covered it, too. "Yeah, a real mess." Without turning or saying anything more he walked away.

We never used the barbecue pit again, although it remained in the yard like blackened ruins of a bombed-out building. The next year, my father drove our tractor fifteen miles to borrow a tar pot (the kind road crews used to heat tar for road repair) from the husband of a woman who patronized my mother's beauty parlor, and towed it fifteen miles to our place. The tar pot made the task of putting an asphalt bottom in the pool easier, but when the pool filled, a greasy scum rose to the top, making the water unfit for swimming. In the fall the brown water remaining in the pool stagnated, and in winter it froze to a beige ice.

A Small Blue Flame

"That Dove is a good driver," my father often said, and he spoke with a conviction in his voice that he didn't reserve for many people. "Dove feels the road. When he comes to a curve he feels the lay of it as he moves into it." He liked to tell about Dove riding a Harley-Davidson motorcycle across the five-mile-long Chesapeake Bay Bridge at ninety-five. "Imagine how narrow that bridge must have looked at that speed," my father marveled. "That boy is a poet at the wheel."

He had less confidence in my Uncle Roger. From our front porch we could hear Roger at least two miles away coming home from work. The evening sun flashed off the windshield of his speeding vehicle as it topped the hill in front of the Hubbard place. We'd hear the tires squeal around the curve near Potter's barn and scream again on the curve by the Custer's house, then the car would burst from behind the row of persimmon trees bordering the road and shoot down the straight toward the end of our lane. Even in the last quarter-mile Roger gunned the car, squeezing the last ounce of thrust from it before skidding into the gravel driveway. "That boy drives like a hungry man tearing down a smoke house with an axe," my father observed one evening as we listened to Roger's approach.

Roger tinkered with cars. Mainly he traded them, always in search of the perfect deal to demonstrate his prowess as a tradesman. He preferred out-of-the-ordinary cars, Studebakers from widows or Packards from retired salesmen, all exceptionally clean and gently used. Once he purchased a 1948 Chrysler New Yorker. You could hardly hear it running, and it rode like an easy chair; but it consumed gasoline at such an alarming rate that Roger chafed at the thought of driving it. "If I tromp down on that car the least little bit," he once complained, "damn, the speedometer goes one way and the gas gauge goes the other; when I slow down, the speedometer comes back but the gas gauge keeps going."

Roger also repaired his cars, but inexpertly, sitting awkwardly on a fender with his feet splayed down in the engine as he monkeyed with a carburetor, or changed spark plugs, or set the points. He wrenched too tightly and stripped threads. He hammered and sweated in all seasons. He dropped small parts and swore loudly as he recovered them caked with grease and dirt. He bullied parts back together when they didn't fit easily and always came up with an extra nut or bolt or odd fragment of metal when the job was finished. His cars were machines to be beaten into submission.

"Lord, Lord," my father once sighed as he listened to the commotion issuing from beneath the raised hood of one of Roger's cars. "Son, if you treat a machine right; it'll treat you right," he once told me. He listened, then shook his head and walked away.

Uncle Roger bought a thirty-eight Packard coupe. He had it parked outside the shed where we kept the tractor and sat bunched up under the hood hammering on a water pump. I slipped beneath the steering wheel to admire the smooth texture of the wheel itself, white as polished bone. Packards were odd cars, overly fancy and from a place other than Fords and Chevys, or Plymouths and Dodges.

"Bang, bang, bang," Roger hammered. The car shook with his movements. I caressed the steering wheel and ran my hands over the leather seats. The musky odor of warm leather filled the car. The chromed horn ring glinted in the sun.

"Bang, bang, bang," sounded Uncle Roger's hammer from under the hood. I pressed the horn ring with the tip of my finger. A long mellow note oozed from the fluted horn behind the grill.

"Bam!" Uncle Roger's head struck against the hood of the car.

"Hey!" he yelled.

I liked the sound of the horn and the result and in a few seconds pressed the ring again — "beeeep."

"Bam!" Uncle Roger's head struck against the hood. "Quit that, dammit!" His voice seemed higher this time, and I felt the car jerk under me.

The bugling of the horn and the thump of Roger's head against the hood provided an enticing staccato of sound.

"Beeeep," I depressed the horn ring a third time.

"Bam," went Roger's head, and the car shook violently as he disengaged his cramped arms and legs from the wires and belts of the engine with the alacrity of a spider fleeing its web before a dust mop.

"Damn you, Billy! Get the hell out of there!" he raged, swinging around the side of the car. He jerked the driver's door open just as I scooted out the opposite side. Beads of sweat hung on his forehead, his graying hair stood up in tufts, and blue smoke curled from his nostrils.

Dove also tinkered with engines. His natural curiosity and desire to fine-tune nagged at him until he'd stop the tractor in mid-field and tear the carburetor down or pull the cap off the distributor to readjust the points. Seeing him stopped on a hill one day when he should have been plowing, my father strolled over to see what was wrong. Dove had small parts scattered over the seat and across the hood.

"It started missing," he explained as my father walked up.

"How much?" my father pressed, slightly piqued at the work delay. He'd had this trouble with Dove before.

"Well, a lot back down the last furrow. It labored on the hill."

"How much?"

"It sputtered like there was dirt in the carburetor."

"How much?"

"Well, twice, I think, but it would have died if I'd kept going."

"Twice! Dammit, Man, I sputter more than that just getting out of bed in the morning! Can't you leave the damn tractor together long enough to plow a damn ten-acre field?"

"I like it better when it runs right."

"Hell, it's running right. One or two misses don't make any difference." My father was good at percentages and believed firmly that a machine running tolerably well should be left alone until it quit altogether. "He who tinkers today will make serious repairs tomorrow," was his credo. "You take a thing apart and it will never go back together just the same as it was," he'd tell me years later when I dismantled parts of my first car, a 1950 Ford, to see what the insides looked like. He was right.

But Dove put the tractor back together with no parts left over, and it ran better than it had for over a year;

even my father said so. Like a musician with perfect pitch, Dove was always adjusting and fine-tuning to achieve perfect harmony. Like my father, he knew that machinery has a soul.

Uncle Roger never discovered more in an automobile than an aggregation of parts. He remained a stranger to machinery, seeking an identity but finding only illusive variety. He brought in Packards, Studebakers, De Sotos, and later a Morris Minor, an English Austin, and a Volkswagen, like a young boy dragging dead animals to be viewed for a while then tossed out.

My father knew about machinery instinctively and maintained a working respect for it. He knew when to make repairs and when coughs and sputters were like sneezes and throat clearings and when they indicated chronic ailments. He trusted machines to run, mainly because he trusted his ability to repair whatever broke, or, if he couldn't easily make the necessary repairs, he could determine the problem and estimate costs; and he knew the right places to take his machinery to have repairs made. He was comfortable around machines and seldom baffled by their complexity; but he was a mechanic, never an engineer.

Dove felt machinery deep inside him, and that's what my father meant when he said that Dove was a poet at the wheel. Riding with him you didn't notice how fast you were traveling because he seemed relaxed, guiding the car with one or both hands. More than that, he studied the road, feeling it through the steering wheel, using the banking of the road to hold the car in a curve. He sensed the constantly changing relationship between the road and the car and never squealed tires or took off too fast or stopped too quickly. He played his car over the road and could do seventy-five or eighty miles an hour, and you'd swear he was doing only fifty.

He never talked much about it, but along with his natural curiosity and his tendency to tinker, something in Dove slipped down into the gears and working parts of his vehicle and swam. He was the first man of genius I ever knew; but he left us, just kind of drove off one day in the summer of 1956 in a turquoise, fifty-three Mercury to take a job as an artificial inseminator of cattle for the Curtis Candy Company, the makers of Baby Ruth candy bars.

"He needed to go," my father said as we watched Dove drive off one Sunday after he'd returned for a visit. The Mercury wound out from the end of our lane and sped up the straight to the curve by the Custer house. The engine slowed then moaned again as Dove aimed down the next straightaway, tires hissing like distant jet engines on the hot pavement. "Notice the way he takes that curve," my father observed as the car moved through the turn near Potter's barn. "Pure poetry," he said, smiling as the miniature car topped the hill by the Hubbard place and hung for a moment like a small blue flame before dropping out of sight.

"God is watching over you," my mother usually affirmed as I departed in my car on a Friday or Saturday evening. She spoke with a confident voice because for her God was a Presence to whom she prayed daily and often spoke aloud to as if He walked beside her. Sometimes she'd reach out and touch my cheek, and I could smell the lilac scent of her favorite hand cream. She'd smile and wave from the front porch steps as I pulled away.

"Drive carefully," my father cautioned, his hands gripping the window sill of my car. He'd never subscribed to my mother's faith and held a deep distrust of all teenage boys. At the cement plant where he worked the relentless motto was, "Safety First," and he'd seen several of his friends and co-workers killed or badly injured in accidents with machines. "Remember," he'd urge, "your car's a projectile. At ninety miles an hour you only have about ten pounds of weight on each wheel, not enough for much control — think about it."

I gave half an ear to his warnings, remembering my role as a pallbearer at Billy Wayne Booth's funeral a few years earlier. Billy Wayne had been riding with his bother, J.E., when their car careened into an orchard at eight-five, throwing Billy Wayne through the windshield. He lay in the orchard for over an hour, gritting his teeth and clutching at handfuls of grass. "The moon was real bright," J.E. told us afterwards, "and I heard the ambulance coming from way off, and I thought it would never get there."

A Scent of Lilacs

In 1959 Steve Frantz's father sold the light blue, forty-nine Chevrolet he'd allowed Steve to drive and bought a black, fifty-seven Ford Fairlane, a two-door sedan with white-walled tires and swept-back aerials. Its flared tail fins and gold stripes insinuated speed. The car ran well, but Steve was a highly strung boy of eighteen, tall and lanky, with unruly brown hair, blue eyes, and thick glasses. He liked reading and writing poetry more than he liked tinkering with automobiles. Listening nervously to every throb in the car's engine, he convinced himself that the new machine was a lemon.

"Man, this car is sick," Nick Firestone groaned one afternoon as he and Steve left the school parking lot and raced the Ford down Route 220 toward Roanoke. At seventy-five its V-8 engine sputtered, and sooty black smoke boiled from its dual exhausts. "Look at that," Nick teased, "this car wouldn't out-drag a loaded semi up-hill." As he spoke his lips curved back into a sneer and his high voice squeezed to a gnat-like whine.

At nineteen Nick had adopted a cynical air to compensate for his small, wiry body. With his thin, sallow face and baby-fine hair, narrowing to a witch's tip, he looked older and tried to speak in controlled, knowing tones as if he were always on the verge of divulging rare secrets. Nick drove a burnt-copper, fifty-three Oldsmobile, handed down to him from an uncle. To see across the steering wheel he sat on a pillow and positioned his seat all the way forward. "I need to be close to my work," he liked to say as he tapped the handle of a billy club he kept on a bracket beneath the dashboard.

None of us believed that the boys in Vinton actually threatened Nick and hurled rocks at his car when he drove there to meet his girlfriend. We also doubted the effectiveness of the gadgetry he constantly ordered for his car to increase its power. But if pressed for the truth on any given subject, Nick spun away, leaving long black scars in stretches of asphalt. He liked winding his car out until its Rocket V-8 engine and automatic transmission screamed with raw power.

Influenced by Nick, Steve sent the Ford to a local garage. John Coble studied beneath the hood, cocking his head to one side as he listened to the laboring engine. He smiled, rebuilt the carburetor, and fine-tuned the machine with fingers as deft as a surgeon's. Steve retrieved his car late of a Friday afternoon and sprinted it up and down Route 11 through Troutville. "It runs better, don't you think?"

"Yeah," Nick mused in a small, cunning voice. "This might do very well. We'll have to try it out."

That evening we drove into Roanoke through all the local drive-ins — the Tally-Ho at the north end of Williamson Road, Toots, halfway down Williamson, well into the city limits, then through Yoda's on the south side of town, where the giant statue of a smiling little kid in black pants and a red and white checkered T-shirt held a giant hamburger toward the road. At every haunt Steve eased the Ford through rows of parked cars in a ritual American promenade of boys and machines.

"Say, let's go out to Sunnyside." Nick spoke in his usual croon. He elbowed me and winked. "We ought to see what this thing'll do, don't you think?"

"I don't know." Steve adjusted himself in his seat uneasily. "It's late."

"Hey, it's almost on the way home. We could zip over to Sunnyside, give it a run, and come straight back to Troutville. Forty-five minutes, tops!"

"I don't see any point in it," Steve returned.

"The point is to see how fast this car will go. Hell, a man can't trust his car until he knows what it'll do. My car'll do one-twenty, no sweat. Now, you want to know if this Ford will take my Olds."

"Not really."

"Sure you do."

"I'm not interested right now." Steve jerked the car through Yoda's exit and back into the street.

"Right." Nick spat out the window, then turned to me. "What do you think? Want to give'er a try?"

"I'm not sure," I said. After three hours over the center hump of the Ford's bulky transmission, I was tired of riding and didn't want to take sides.

Steve squirmed in his seat, revving the engine in neutral at a red light. The engine torque rocked the car gently with each pressure on the accelerator.

"Maybe. Do you think we should?" He glanced over at me.

"It's your car. You decide." I was feeling a little trapped. I hadn't liked driving at high speeds since Billy Wayne had died. I'd seen the twisted car with its shattered windshield and smears of dried blood in the seat and wondered if his life had flashed before him like people said it did in those last desperate moments.

"Yeah, you want to try." Nick lowered his voice to a whisper. "But you're chicken."

"All right," Steve consented under his breath and spun out as the light turned green. Sunnyside, a two-mile stretch of straight road, known for late-night drag races, lay at least forty miles away, just west of Fincastle.

We drove the length of Williamson, past Toots again, down Boxley Hill past the city limit sign, then by the Tally-Ho and the Planter's Peanut store where the tall statue of a dapper Mr. Peanut in a top hat and tails smiled cynically through his monocle.

Away from the street lights the moon shined on the mountains. The car purred in the evening cool, its tires swishing quietly over the road. We could feel the power through the floorboard and seats and hear it in the rumble of the dual exhausts.

Eight miles farther north, at Crossroads, Steve eased the car over the four lanes of Route 11 and onto the two lanes of Route 220. We swept through three miles of apple and peach orchards in full bloom to a narrow street looping past two run-down apartment buildings known as Daleville Academy. Nick liked driving this street with his left foot on the brake and his right on the accelerator, to make his Olds labor until the rumble of its exhausts cracked against the brick buildings and wide-eyed children turned to stare.

We passed Hilltop Tavern and dropped down a long, graceful hill through rolling pastures enclosed by white fences; then on through Fincastle itself, down the hill and around the curve to the bridge with arched steel girders which marked the beginning of Sunnyside straight.

"We'd better check for the law," Nick urged, his voice so tense with excitement I could feel the pulse of his heartbeat.

"Yeah," Steve agreed. He drove slowly along the two mile stretch. The dash lights illuminated his pale face and thick glasses and highlighted Nick's cocky smile. From my seat in the middle I watched the small ring on the hood ornament ride above the pavement like a gun sight in search of a target.

We traversed the two miles easily, the car rising and falling over the road like a hawk riding gentle irregularities of air. Mist, phosphorescent in moonlight, hovered low in the fields, reminding me of pictures in old books I discovered in Aunt Betty's attic, of horses pulling hay wagons down winding roads that crossed streams and curved away into murky distances.

"Now, let's see what she'll do!" Nick said, breaking the silence at the end of the straight.

"Right," Steve replied. His voice cracked and he trembled beside me. He turned the car around and brought it to a standstill and sat for a moment, gunning the engine and staring blankly across the hood at the road.

"Go!" Nick yelled. His voice snapped in the air like a whip. Steve jerked in the seat.

"Right!" He jammed the accelerator to the floor. The car snarled and shot forward, its engine straining, shaking the car as it rammed from first gear quickly into second, then through a long, almost reluctant surge into high. Air moaned through the carburetor. The broken center line in the road flickered then streamed by in a smooth ribbon of white. Wind kyried around the door and window seams, and the engine and transmission screamed. The car hurtled over the road, its black tail fins slicing the air like wings.

"Slow down! Slow down! The bridge has to be right up ahead!" I finally managed to blurt out, gripping the seat and curved dashboard.

"No it ain't! No it ain't!" Nick's voice was smooth and tight as he craned his neck across me to see the speedometer. "Keep goin'! Keep goin'! We're doing a hundred and fifteen! It'll do one-twenty! Keep goin'!"

Steve sat transfixed, his hands locked on the steering wheel, his eyes glued to the road, and his mouth partly open as if he were about to scream.

"No!" I yelled, forcing a reply to Nick's urging.

Suddenly, the bridge was there; its girders rose like ladders out of the fog hanging above the creek. Steve jerked his foot to the brake. The car immediately skidded out of control. He tried to wrestle it back into the road, but it careened across both lanes. He grimaced, clenched the steering wheel in both hands and bowed his head.

"Shit!" Nick hissed under his breath and placed both hands on the dashboard and shoved himself back into the seat as though trying to will away the on-coming bridge. I saw them give up then ducked my head, closed my eyes and waited.

"Oh, God!" someone moaned in a tight voice, like a question, as the car began to roll. It crashed through the darkness, throwing us wildly against the doors, head-liner, dashboard and seats, tumbling us in a maze of arms and legs before coming to rest on its side a few yards away from the bridge, steam hissing furiously from its radiator.

"Hell, it's gonna blow up!" Nick yelled, bruising the inside of my thigh with the heel of his shoe as he clambered over us and up through the heavy passenger door: it fell back on its latch with a thud.

112

"Hey!" Steve screamed. He tried to raise the massive door. "Hey! Come back here, you bastard."

"It's gonna blow up!" Nick screamed from the other side of the road.

"We can't get out, dammit!" Steve yelled back. The car was hot and close inside.

"Nick!" Steve called again his voice loud and commanding.

"All right. All right." Nick raced back to the car. We could hear him scramble up the side. The door creaked open. "C'mon! C'mon!" He waited as Steve and I boosted and dragged each other out of the car.

We didn't say anything for a while. Miraculously, except for a charley horse on my thigh, we were unhurt. We just stood looking at the Ford on its side with steam billowing from its front end. The air was heavy with the acrid smells of gasoline and steam and burned rubber mingling oddly with the scent of lilacs drifting from somewhere beyond the road.

"You got us into this," Steve finally growled at Nick. He began to pace back and forth in the gravel near the car.

"The hell I did." Nick's voice seemed suddenly thin and weak.

"Sure you did. This was all your idea."

Nick winced and squatted down on his haunches. "Maybe you could write a poem about it," he finally muttered, but the savvy had gone from his voice.

"I might. I just might. It would beat listening to your harebrained schemes."

A car stopped, and a man we didn't know spoke to us. He looked curious and frightened until he determined that we weren't hurt. Cars began to line up along the road. Some of the people knew Steve and Nick and whispered their names. Calls were made and a state trooper arrived. He examined the car and measured the skid marks: one hundred and twenty-five yards. He stared hard at us and shook his head. "You boys were real lucky. I hope you know that," he said quietly and kept looking at us for a few seconds before turning to write his report.

Nick's older brother, James, came to pick us up. We heard him coming through Fincastle at least a mile away. "Listen! Hear it?" Nick said, cocking his ear toward the sound. We could hear the high-pitched whine of a vehicle approaching at high speed. "That's James. I'd know the sound of that truck anywhere. He took Richard Simmon's fifty-eight Impala in a quarter-mile!"

"Aw, Nick," Steve moaned.

"He did!" Nick shouted, his eyes regaining luster.

"Grow up, Nick! Grow up!" Steve turned, spat on the car and walked to the other side of the bridge.

From Nick's house I drove home in the moonlight with my radio off and entered through the kitchen door and limped carefully down the long, undisturbed hall-way toward my room at the back of the house. I could hear my father breathing heavily in sleep at the far end of the house across from my room. As I passed my mother's room her voice came from the darkness, "You're all right. God loves you." She spoke quietly, emphatically, the way she always did after hours of prayer.

"Yes, Ma'am." I paused near her door. A breeze drifting through her open window and across her bed carried the lilac scent of her hand cream.

"I'm glad you're home," she added quietly, turning in her bed. "I'll see you in the morning."

"Yes, Ma'am." I continued down the hallway to my room, where I undressed without turning on the light and crawled naked into bed and pulled the covers up around my neck. A dog barked in the distance, wind rustled leaves on the pear tree in the back yard, and across the hall my father drew deep, regular breaths. I could still smell my mother's hand cream and fell asleep in the sweet scent of lilacs.

PART THREE

A Promise

In the crisp air and slanting light of mid-October a monarch butterfly appeared at the northern edge of the field through which I was walking. In moments it crossed the expanse and quivered, a mere speck, above the tall grass and brambles beyond the south margin of the field. I watched it disappear; half a mile farther on it would pass through the updrafts rising along the bluffs of the Mississippi River, where towboats shove cumbersome barges through channels and shifting currents.

No one knows for sure why monarchs make their long migration each year. A change in the angle of light against its wings, a hitch in the rhythm of wind may have stirred the one I'd just seen, but before completing its journey it might fly through parts of Missouri, Oklahoma, and Texas, in a wide arc around the Gulf of Mexico, even as far as Mexico City. I imagined the wash from small wing tips against my cheeks and marveled at the strength and perseverance of butterflies on wings as thin as flower petals.

Only two seasons have passed since my son mastered the art of kite flying. He used a medium kite, roughly the shape of a butterfly, playing out his string carefully to keep the tension just right until the kite soared to a small speck in wide empyreal blue.

I remember years of wincing as I watched him stumble along, dragging his kites upside down across the yard until their frames collapsed. "Hold it up! Hold it up!" I'd tell him as he trailed a kite behind him like a piece of heavy rope. With more encouragement he finally learned to run fast enough to loft them into the air and keep them braced against the wind for a few moments. Even so, most flights ended with string and fragments of colored paper dangling from bare trees. But he kept trying until he learned how to gauge the strength of currents and how to feed his kites gracefully into them.

"Can you control it in this much wind?" I asked one day as an ascending kite at the end of his string veered sharply to the left and plunged perilously downward for a moment.

"Oh, sure," he responded, tugging the string until the kite climbed, regained its balance and held steady.

He has come a long way from the mechanical mobile that once hung above his crib. The device consisted of four large plastic butterflies suspended from a music box that played a spare version of "Rock-a-Bye-Baby." Fascinated, he babbled happily, straining toward the bright, plastic forms twisting and turning in their mock flight while the small box cycled relentlessly through its song. But I couldn't help feeling sorry for him as he batted away at aimless forms.

He has grown. He feels the pulses and rhythms in the wind, and the mechanics of kite flying no longer entangle him; the thin cord arcing up to the kite has left its imprint in his fingers.

I've watched him test the wind through the vibrations in the string, knowingly, instinctively. I stood nearby one day as he played out all his available line, even adding scraps of string from another supply, until the kite soared steadily above the rougher currents shuttling among hills and trees.

"How do you know you can keep it that high?" I asked, to see what he'd say.

"I'm not sure," he laughed, "I just know!" The kite was barely visible, a small speck shining in the sunlight, when he began to reel it in. He worked carefully, steadily for nearly twenty minutes before it hovered just above his head, gracefully, like a giant butterfly returning from a distant place to feed at his hands.

Follow Through

In all the years my father and I hunted ruffed grouse together we never discovered an easy route to the hunting grounds on the far side of Tinker Mountain. The climb up the steep trail was part of a cycle and rite of passage. Most farmers didn't take the time to hunt, but my father had always made the time. He told me that one year, when he was a young man, the hunting season had opened for forty-five days and he'd gone hunting forty-five times. His need to hunt lay deep in primitive instincts, awakened each fall and nourished by long excursions across Tinker Mountain. For companionship he took me and a liver-and-white English Pointer named Champion.

On the south side of the mountain it didn't seem to matter that fences needed mending and shocks of corn lay rotting in the field, or that we hadn't put up enough hay to last through the winter and would have to buy feed from a neighbor. Across Tinker Mountain we couldn't hear the loose sheets of tin pounding on the barn roof when the wind blew or hear the steady moan of the cement plant where my father had finally taken a job to supplement his income; nor could we see the corrosive white dust uncoiling from the plant etching the land for miles across the valley.

Hunting mattered. It had a purpose and clearly defined rules. Once we had climbed the mountain and descended into the silent hollows on the south side, our relationship turned on mutual concern for one another's safety and a simple code — shoot birds only on the wing, make clean kills, and count only what goes into the bag.

We picked up the trail leading across the mountain among clusters of scrub oaks, tangled patches of blackberry vines, broom sedge, and rocks under the power line where only the faintest impressions of a pathway survived. Three hundred yards up from the power line, we found clearer signs of a trail near a spring at the base of the mountain. We cleaned out the leaves and let the water clear before drinking. A few yards above the spring, the trail began its ascent in earnest. We climbed over shelves of rock and through a series of sharp turns and several narrow cuts overhung with laurel and running straight up the mountain. My father climbed in long easy strides, stopping at turns or level places to wait for me. "This'll tone up your mountain legs and get your hunting blood up," he often claimed.

The trail up the mountain connected with the Appalachian Trail at the top. We followed this trail, which veered south just after the intersection, down to a wide expanse of fields and thickets called Lambert's Meadow. It spread across a long hollow rising westward for nearly a mile. We commenced our hunt there in the cold gray morning light in frost heavy enough to make the leaves crackle under our feet. We jumped grouse among clusters of fox grape vines bordering the meadow, usually singles, but sometimes in feeding parties of four or five.

"Keep moving," my father frequently instructed. "If the dog makes a stand, don't stop; work up next to him and make him hold till you're ready."

Lambert's Meadow terminated between two knobs, Julie's Knob on the right and McAfee's Knob on the left. We turned south again, climbed still higher across

McAfee's Knob, as the mid-morning sun melted the frost, and hunted just below the crest of Catawba Mountain, through more wild grape vines and thickets, toward several abandoned fields. My father hunted higher in the mountain, waving the dog and me down into the thicker vines where grouse were more likely to feed. "Watch the dog, now; keep him in close," he'd call if he saw me slackening my pace. He'd maintain voice contact, even if he couldn't see me. "If a grouse gets up wild, keep your eyes on him so we can follow him," he'd say, his voice controlled just under a yell. "He'll sit tighter when we find him again."

We reached the fields and began circling down into the long, rolling hollows, hunting eastward through the flats around Carvin's Cove, the main water supply for the city of Roanoke only a few miles away. There, in the heat of the late morning sun, mist often rose from the marshes.

On these extended hunts my father always led the way, his Model 12 Winchester shotgun cradled in his right arm, his right hand lightly cupping the pistol grip in the stock. Remarkable for its trim design and invisible hammer, the gun had been purchased by my grandmother in 1913 as a gift for my grandfather. He hunted with it for years then handed it on to my father who smiled, claiming that by the time he'd inherited the gun it was so well trained it leaped to his shoulder on its own when a grouse or covey of quail flew up. Over the years the safety button at the front of the trigger guard grew too small for his bulbous index finger, so he whittled down a copper penny with a pair of side-cutting pliers and soldered it to the button. Thereafter, every time he

prepared to shoot he pressed the scarred profile of
Abraham Lincoln on the copper chip.

A lead pellet, still visible as a hard, blue-black kernel,
lay just under the skin between the first and second
knuckles of the index finger on my father's right hand.
When he cradled the shotgun he extended that finger
along the stock for balance.

I watched him in his faded hunting coat and cap,
moving through the underbrush and trees, speaking to
the dog in a quiet voice, waving him out or calling him
in. He taught me how to work the dog to find game, how
to make the dog retrieve a downed bird without damag-
ing it. He taught me how to make clean kills. "Move your
gun in long sweeping strokes the way an artist uses a
paintbrush," he once explained to me after I'd missed
several shots at birds quartering to the left or right.
"When a grouse gets up follow him with your sight until
after you pass him, but don't stop to shoot; keep your
gun moving just ahead of him until after you've
squeezed off the shot — learn to follow through."

Grouse seldom fed in the flats around the cove, but
we found quail there. Once, we hunted the grassy fields
just after a rain. The sun burned through and fog gathered into low banks propelled by light wind currents.
The dog was working a stretch of thicket in the far corner
of a field. "He's found a covey," my father called and
moved quickly toward the dog. As he neared him a
blanket of mist crept over them. I heard him speak to the
dog — "Steady!" I heard the birds get up and watched
them fly out of the mist toward a dark row of trees. I saw
the burst of flame from the end of my father's gun barrel.
The lead bird buckled and fell — a clean kill. My father
emerged partly from the mist, pumped the gun with a

sharp, quick motion, then aimed and fired again, downing a second bird. He stood back for a moment, with a strange, wide-eyed expression, trying to locate me in the traveling fog. Seeing me in the east corner of the field, he turned back to speak to the dog as the mist rolled in again, obscuring them from my view a second time. For a moment, in the silence that followed, I felt an emptiness, as if my father had suddenly vanished into the blankness around the edges of a dream. I closed my eyes to shake off the illusion and could see only darkness with a small beam of light holding in the center of it.

We hunted the flats along the north side of the cove for over two miles until we came to a trail that wound back up the south side of the mountain. We followed this trail into the lower hollows, stopping for lunch on a low shelf of rock where the trail curved sharply west and crossed a small stream. I always felt tired at this point and dreaded the long pull back up the mountain. We built a fire and ate our lunches, cold turkey sandwiches and hunks of fruitcake during the holiday season, washing them down with water from the stream. Even the dog rested with us while we ate.

My father once killed a grouse a few yards into the laurel thicket just on the other side of the stream. He'd stepped into the woods to relieve himself, but, having learned from years of hunting never to leave his shotgun out of reach in the woods, he'd taken it with him and stood holding it with one hand, loosely, upside down across his shoulder when the grouse flew up a few yards in front of him. He must have been holding the shotgun with his left hand around the pistol grip, his index finger already resting on the trigger guard, for by the time I heard the whir of wings and turned in the direction of the sound, he'd already aimed, pointing the gun like a pistol. He fired once and the grouse dropped. Confident of the shot, he simply flipped the gun back to his shoulder and continued his business.

After lunch we worked our way slowly back up the gentle slopes, taking a final rest on a massive rock jutting out from the crest of Tinker Mountain above our farm. From this vantage point we could see for miles northward up the Valley of Virginia and watch the sun begin its decline beyond the two knobs to the west. From the rock our farm looked clean, and the holes in the barn roof didn't look so big.

My father never told me how he'd gotten the lead pellet in his finger. He said it was a number six shot, the result of a shooting accident when he was a young man. But when I pressed him to tell me the story he always turned away and said he'd explain it to me some other time. He never did.

I now live in the Midwest where there are no ruffed grouse, so I seldom use my father's shotgun for hunting. But I tell my son stories, and in late October when the angle of light decreases and the air turns colder, I lift the gun from its cabinet, wipe away the dust and oil the metal parts to keep them from rusting. Sometimes, after cleaning the gun, I throw it to my shoulder and dry-fire it. I imagine a grouse flying away from me, quartering to the right or to the left. I imagine following the bird until the brass bead on the end of the barrel glides just in front of it, but I don't stop to shoot. I keep the gun moving as I squeeze the trigger and feel the small vibration deep inside its breech mechanism as the hammer spring releases and the hammer strikes against the firing pin.

Guppies in a Gas Pump

Back in the early fifties, had you been looking for Hogan's store, I would have directed you to pick up State Route 779 near Daleville, where it departed from U.S. 220 and began wandering in a westward direction, roughly paralleling Tinker Mountain for six or seven miles until, having passed through the cement plant near the foot of Julie's Knob, it turned sharply south and crossed Catawba Creek on a rusty iron bridge.

I would have warned you about the turn leading to the bridge. Route 779 was a dirt road then, listed as unimproved and you would have had to brake hard because the turn was sharp and because of potholes in the low side of the ramp leading to the bridge.

Your approach to the store on the south side of the creek would have been announced by the clatter of wooden planks against the cross members of the bridge and by the yawn and stir of several dogs drowsing in the shade. At the end of the bridge you would have passed beneath the branches of a giant sycamore, and in the heat of a summer's day you would have smelled its strong musk.

The ramshackle store, on the edge of what might have seemed a wilderness to any stranger, stood not more than fifty yards from the bridge and was the last such convenience for at least twenty miles. The building was little more than a clapboard box with a square front that rose slightly higher than the gabled roof, an unconvincing attempt to make the building appear larger than it was.

A single doorway centered in the front of the store served as the only way in or out. Through most of the year this passageway stood loosely covered by an ill-fitting screen door held to by a long, thin spring. The lightly galvanized mesh had grown dark and gossamer from years of rust. The words of the slogan "Rainbo is Good Bread," stenciled across the upper section of the screen, were barely recognizable, and the abbreviated rainbow that had once curved beneath them had eroded to a small fraction of a yellowed arc.

An overhang, jutting out from the front of the store like a huge, square lip, extended just far enough across the dirt driveway to allow a single automobile to pass under its cover.

The two supporting pillars rested on a concrete slab. A large, green container of coal oil for lamps and heaters sat near the right pillar, and an ancient gasoline pump stood near the left. You would have recognized it, one of those tall, round pumps with a long handle for lifting the amber liquid to the glass tank at the top, where the amount registered against black numbers from 1 to 10 on a metal rack inside. To extract the liquid, you simply unhooked a hose hanging in a loop near the bottom of the glass container and drained the gasoline into the tank of your car. Originally the pump had been bright red, but the paint had faded; and years of weather had also caused the finish to crack and wrinkle, until the pump's surface looked like dried harness leather.

The proprietor's full name was Katherine Hogan, but everyone who frequented the store knew her as Aunt Kate. Like her store Aunt Kate was unencumbered by affectations and frills. I don't remember her ever wearing anything but loose-fitting print dresses, the kind often crafted from cotton feed sacks, usually light blue, soft green, or pure white and peppered with small flowers. Throughout the year she also wore heavy cotton stockings rolled to just below her knees, and while she sometimes wore black shoes she preferred a pair of faded cloth slippers, especially in the warmer months. She attempted to keep her gray hair tied back in a bun, but most of the time it flew loosely around her ears and neck.

In good weather she sat outside, her battered rush-bottomed chair positioned near the southeast corner of the store. From this vantage point she could watch both the road and the end of the bridge. Typically, she sat with her left arm across her stomach, her left hand gently cupping the elbow of her right arm. She kept the fingers of her right hand tucked under her chin, but in quieter moments, they crept out and began working slowly across her lips with the measured movements of an indolent butterfly exploring a flower.

Aunt Kate maintained her daily vigil religiously, squinting against the morning sun and waving off flies as she napped through long, warm afternoons. To steady her contemplations she dipped snuff, leaning forward now and then to expel the waste into the dust near her chair. Most of the time she acknowledged passersby, but obliquely, by lifting her right hand or a couple of fingers briefly away from her face, a gesture that only farm folk who knew her would have seen or expected.

I knew her as a trader in "co-cola" and nickel cakes, banana flavored ones with raisins on top and a cream filling in the center, which she grudgingly swapped for empty pop bottles my friends and I collected from ditches along the road during our Sunday bike rides. On a good Sunday we could earn upwards of fifty cents, but

Aunt Kate always figured the bottles were hers anyway, because, as she frequently explained, "them boys up at the concrete plant, they carry them bottles off all the time, and they don't never pay no deposit." If she were in a good mood, however, she'd pay us the two cents per bottle; if not, she might allow us the mean compensation of a single bottle of pop and a nickel cake for twenty or so bottles. On such occasions we chose RCs or NEHIs because they were bigger.

Aunt Kate's adult customers fared better on the whole than her younger barterers. But since they had little to select from, besides gasoline and coal oil, flour, fatback, salt, sugar, and navy beans, their visits were generally brief and uncomplicated. Aunt Kate transacted most of her business from her chair, often making small change from one of the deep pockets of her dress. A quiet banter accompanied some purchases, but most were conducted with a wry cordiality and an economy of language and movement.

Life around Aunt Kate advanced with the cadence of dust accumulating on window panes or rust particles falling from her screen door. She required few amenities, rejected gimmicks, and seldom made promises. For years, however, you could be certain of finding Aunt Kate in her chair, and while the planks on the bridge made an awful racket when a vehicle crossed, they seemed never to wear out.

But that was some years back. A wide paved road now begins a gracefully banked curve almost on the exact spot where Aunt Kate's store stood, and State Route 779 crosses Catawba Creek on a concrete bridge that gleams so white in the sun it makes your eyes water. You need hardly slow down for the turn at all, and the road is probably listed as improved secondary.

Now, too, you can ease onto Interstate 70 near St. Louis, just down the road a piece from where I live, and ride all the way to Denver and beyond and never move your steering wheel more than five degrees to the left or right of center. Nearly halfway across this distance, among groves of garish signs — yellow arches, giant steers, fifteen-foot acronyms, twenty-foot cowboy hats and tilted buckets — you will pass a special place boasting uniqueness and haute cuisine.

The building is sheathed in laminated wood siding, tinted Williamsburg Gray. It sits in a spacious parking lot studded with small birch trees. Double red doors, appointed with large brass knobs, wide strap hinges, and heavy brass coach lamps, mark the entryway.

Inside, the walls and ceilings are textured to appear rough-hewn. Here patrons walk on wood floors coated with polyurethane. Wagon wheels fashioned into gleaming chandeliers hang from uniformly carved beams. Ox yokes decorate door lintels. Snaffle bits shine from corner posts, and plowshares, pinned to wood-grained walls like crippled wings, accent a filigree of hames and singletrees. In various alcoves and crannies, old wooden sleighs, plow beams, wooden boxes, hand-cranked mills, and oiled harness sets are displayed in carefully disheveled attitudes. Here and there, too, you may see your reflection in mirrors mounted in horse collars.

Yet more striking, in the foyer leading to the main dining area — where young hostesses, smiling in long white dresses, glide from behind clumps of exotic plants to greet you with pleasantries and request, "How many?" — you may also notice, behind the waitress station, one of those tall gas pumps, standing like a lighthouse in a jungle and newly painted a glossy red. A light shines at the top of the glass tank, which has been converted into an aquarium. Bubbles escape from beneath a plastic sunken ship, resting bow down in the sand, and artificial seaweed sways faintly with their passing.

You may stand in the gentle breeze wafting from an overhead fan and marvel at such chic recycling and the bug-eyed guppies circling, circling, darting up, darting down, pausing to stare out at you through the ghost of your reflection, then circling again to chase those golden bubbles rising through the gallon marks.

I heard its roar before I saw it appear at the top of the curve near the Custer place and could see my uncles and aunts and cousins laughing and cheering over the cattle frames as it lumbered down toward the end of our lane. I waved from the concrete dam along the north side of the pool and they waved back. My father's bare arm flashed from the window.

He liked that truck. He could sit high in the cab and command the road, and folks knew who he was. He didn't mind that horse hair stuck out from its torn seat or that its top and short hood were caved in and its fenders badly dented. It didn't seem to matter that the truck periodically sputtered and died because dirt clogged the fuel line. He carried a wrench and tire pump, and when the truck stalled he disconnected the fuel line from the carburetor and blew the dirt back into the fuel tank. He got used to the procedure and accepted it as part of the normal operation of the machine, like gassing it up or changing the oil.

But it ground to a halt one day in the driveway just across from the spring house under a full load of hay. Bearings lay scattered along the dirt road like the spawn of Leviathan in a dry stream bed. He just seemed to give up on the truck. He hooked the tractor to it, pulled it to the barn, unloaded it, and shoved it under the pecan tree. It sat for two years, collecting spider webs and mud dauber nests, until Dewey Wood traded him four shoats and twenty dollars for it.

Call Me Ishmael

Not long ago I purchased a used pickup truck, a white half-ton with a short bed, gold striping, and over-sized tires. Parked, it sits casually with its bed slightly raked. I imagine it at rest. Not many years ago it might have been a dapple-gray gelding (it has only six cylinders) slouched at a hitching post near a wide veranda. Now, when I escape the gridded parking lot where I work to cruise country byways, the ram's head on the end of the hood glides above the road like a ship's figurehead plowing through smooth water.

Colleagues smile. "When are you going to get a gun rack for the rear window?" one asks. "Why do you need a truck?" others query. "Do you really need a truck?" the wife of one of my co-workers questioned me one day in that modulated and accusatory tone usually reserved for young sons who've discovered motorcycles too early.

Need, of course, is relative. I like my truck primarily for its looks and because it's just shy of acceptable, even a little menacing, among all those look-alike foreign and domestic models that school in the parking lot where I work.

"How do you like your new car?" I asked a friend one evening as I walked him from our front door to the curb where his gold BMW waited.

"Oh, it's OK," he replied, "but it doesn't have the power for passing I'd like. I'm doing a little market research for something better."

A week or so later I saw him driving a red car, a Honda, I think; I couldn't really tell because so many of those small, high-backed, grill-less and slope-fronted jobs look alike to me. A few years ago Triumph called it "the shape of things to come." They were right: modern automobile designers follow one another like ducklings in a row, waddling resolutely and urgently toward a murky pond. Maybe that's a function of a throw-away economy; selling has become the main point, and it's easier to hawk an imaginary uniqueness than take the time and energy to develop distinctive character.

That wasn't always so. In the forties and fifties, even into the sixties, Ford, General Motors, and Chrysler products, automotive meat and potatoes where I grew up, were at least distinguishable, even among themselves. Pontiac hoods sported Indian heads; Chevrolets did not. Pontiacs also carried ribbed chrome strips down their hoods and trunks. Buicks were larger, with chromed louvers in the sides of their hoods and front fenders. Oldsmobiles looked sad. Mercurys were bigger than Fords, and fancier. Plymouths and Dodges, smaller than Chryslers and De Sotos, were sturdy but nondescript and usually owned by grandparents or old maid aunts. Lincolns and Cadillacs existed in a world of their own.

There were others: Kaisers, Frasers, Hudsons, and Nashes, long and boat-like, were generally shunned, probably because everyday folk associated those shapes with hard-shelled critters that ravage fields and gardens. Studebakers and Henry J's were tolerated like shy relatives with weak chins. Random Packards drifted through the countryside like sharks on the prowl.

I didn't do market research when I bought my truck. I saw it on a lot and horse-traded for it. That used to be the way of the land, and my trading instincts and affections for automobiles are rooted in 1950s southern Virginia where most folk bargained for cars and extended their personalities through the character of their vehicles. A man was known by the automobile he kept. "Oh, you know B.J. Price," someone might say. "He drives a Blue Ford." For more emphasis a model and date might be included — "Yeah, I know ol' Jake Saunders, know'd him for years. Drives that black, forty-eight Chevy coupe, don't he?"

Special cars fetched even more elaborate descriptions. Lina Lee Ashby drove a fifty-six De Soto, Fire-Dome V-8. This more precise designation recognized a psychological complexity knitting car and driver, a demure school teacher who had never married and who rarely spoke outside her classroom. Her De Soto was a dusky green, the color of deep tropical water. Cream stripes extended like tails of comets from the front fenders to the trailing edges of the wide tail fins. The machine began and ended with massive chrome bumpers and carried a filigree of chrome that glinted in the sun.

The car's matching interior swaddled Lina Lee in luxury. Its seats were dark green trimmed in a lighter shade. Plush pile carpet covered the floor. Multiple dials and gauges on the dashboard lay enmeshed in chrome and the instrument panel glowed at night with the pastel hue of continuous fireflies on a summer evening.

With its huge engine, power brakes, power steering, and push-button drive, the car moved by erotic surges and pulses, activated by the slightest suggestion of pressure. It skimmed over the asphalt like a dawn wind caressing meadow flowers. It raised eyebrows and piqued imaginations. Lina Lee exulted at the center of wide-spread attention and gripped the steering wheel with both hands. Onlookers could only speculate on the flight of mid-life fancy impelling her from the thirty-nine Dodge she had driven for sixteen years into the De Soto. She drove her new machine with a wry smile, as if she were aware of secrets that awed bystanders could only guess at.

Automobiles also separated classes and revealed different attitudes among them. Mrs. Arthur Jenvey, the wife of a retired Caterpillar executive, drove a long, steel gray, thirty-nine Buick, usually down the middle of the road. A stern, humorless woman, she never laughed openly. On rare occasions when a comment or situation amused her, a single large "Ha" escaped from her slightly parted lips while her expression remained fixed as death. Farm workers and day laborers cut for the shoulders to avoid her stony countenance and the grim, slatted grill of her Buick.

Less advantaged folk operated older cars, usually acquired through arrangements behind barns, in the back yards of dilapidated houses, or in derelict garages. Occasionally, they'd turn sorrowful eyes on new widows and speed away in sleek Chevys or Fords, and once in a while, in a Pontiac, a Buick, or a Mercury. More often, they prowled junk yards in search of parts, and when a car died they shoved it to the back yard or into a ditch, its hood still raised as if gasping for breath.

I first discovered the semblance between character and vehicle during the years I waited for the school bus at the end of our lane. On warm spring mornings Clyde Ashworth's black forty-nine, Buick-Eight wallowed though the turn and dynaflow-moaned up the slight grade toward my waiting place. A retired insurance salesman, Clyde drove his car slowly and self-consciously. Its wide, smiling grill suited this easy-going, overweight man whose gentleness seemed always a trifle labored and too smooth, even on those summer mornings when he brought his wife to my mother's beauty parlor and waited outside in his car, chewing tobacco and spitting the excess into a one-pound coffee can.

At 7:30 each school day, my fourth grade teacher, Miss Harris, burst from the low glare of the morning sun and down the grade on her way to Asbury Elementary in her fifty-two Chevrolet, an ivory coupe with a gray top and plain black tires. A stately middle-aged woman with dark eyes and long, gray-streaked auburn hair curling around her oval face, Miss Harris sat high in the seat. She'd glance in my direction and wave, her expression always quizzical and a little sad. Then she'd turn her eyes back to the road and whisk quietly by in powerglide.

'Am Elbert drove a plain forty-nine Studebaker pickup. In spite of a church that frowned on vehicles other than black, 'Am's truck was light blue, a concession to his flair for business. The truck whined gracefully through the turn and purred up the grade. The horizontal slits in its grill led the way in a determined expression, half grin/half grimace, and 'Am operated the truck the way he handled all his machinery, with resolute steadiness, always business-like and focused as though in pursuit of some special goal known only to himself.

Ed Selander crafted boilers for steam locomotives at the Norfolk and Western shops in Roanoke. In 1955 it still hadn't occurred to him that his profession was nearly obsolete. He was a large, uncomplicated man, gentle and plain, yet muscular and hard as the sheets of steel he curved and riveted into boilers.

For years Ed traveled the twenty miles from his home in Mount Union to Roanoke in a murky green, forty-nine Ford pickup. Typically, he sat behind the wheel with a vacant look in his eyes, until he saw someone he knew. His face then widened into a broad smile, his lips parted, and a soft, wet "Hi," like water dripping into damp cotton, issued from deep within his throat. Even if you couldn't actually hear the greeting you'd know it was there as certain as sunlight beaming through a southern window on a clear day.

You could tell that truck, too. Its grill was like Ed's smile, broad and pleasing as the vehicle floated over the asphalt, breathing air to cool its quiet, flat-headed V-8 engine. Idling, the engine made almost no sound. At higher speeds it produced more RPMs, but not significantly more noise. Still, you'd know it was Ed's truck because it produced that clear high-pitched sound, as if somewhere down in its inner gears and bearings a wizened elf pumped air through a small silver whistle.

Dewey Wood chugged steadily through the curve and up the grade every morning at 7:40 in his Model A Ford. Dressed in khaki work clothes and a baggy engineer's cap with a long shovel bill, Wood sat so low in the car that only his head showed above the steering wheel, which he gripped firmly near the top with both hands as if he were afraid of losing control.

He maintained that no other vehicle could be trusted, even though over the years he had repaired and rebuilt the Ford so often that little besides the chassis remained of the original. New, the car must have been blue with black fenders, but the initial color had oxidized to a mottled brown with hints of color in splotches along its sides.

Wood had been a robust man in his younger days, but l ike his car, his health had slowly faded. He made his living as a carpenter, probably because he felt secure with malleable wood, yet he clung to his small farm, working the red clay soil with a team of horses and worn-out machinery, which he'd gathered from farmers who'd pastured their horses and bought tractors.

On at least three occasions Wood's horses had run away with him, and each time some broken part failed to heal properly, leaving him further diminished. In his last accident he'd been dragged nearly half a mile clinging to a mowing machine before he managed to stop the rampaging horses. After that he walked with a crab-like gait, one shoulder lower than the other, and he was smaller in stature.

On one of the last mornings that I remember seeing Dewey Wood, his Model A rounded the curve, the gurgle of its engine deepening as the vehicle entered the grade. No face appeared in the windshield, and the car moved aimlessly toward my waiting place, as if it had finally taken its own head and was moving wide-eyed toward some distant adventure.

Only as the vehicle drew to within a few yards of where I stood did I see the two gnarled hands gripping the wheel. The shovel-billed cap, barely visible above the rolled-down side window, dipped slightly and a skinny index finger lifted briefly from the wheel as the car churned by. It hung for a moment, a dark silhouette in the morning sun, before vanishing into the vapor rising from the pavement.

A couple of years ago a friend of mine, a college professor, bought a new white Honda Accord, because, he said, his consumer magazine rated it highly. A few weeks later a neighbor who runs a bookstore bought a gray-blue Honda Accord. Not long after that a second neighbor who works with computers also purchased a gray-blue Honda Accord. A month later the lady who runs a Guest House on the college campus nearby passed me in a new Honda Accord, a gray blue one. At one point six Honda Accords regularly cruised the neighborhood, five of them gray-blue. Such repetition makes character-ization difficult; you can't say to someone, "Oh, you know Phil, and Ken, and Bob, and Frank, and Sally, and Tom, they drive gray-blue Honda Accords." Of course, if asked, all these folk would explain that blue was the only color available and that the Honda Accord is highly rated by *Car and Driver, Consumer Reports,* etc. Perhaps the complexity of our lives demands that we do market research and more and more seek the advice of experts to make basic decisions — where to eat, what to eat, what films to see, what diets to choose, what vehicles to buy. With the help of experts, maybe our lives, like gray-blue Honda Accords, can be acceptable, safe, comfortable, uniform, and impervious to criticism. But I wonder about the shape of things to come. Mornings, as I head across the slotted parking lot toward my office, I often glance back; among so many muted grills my truck looks like Moby Dick in a school of minnows.

Ritual

He's found a car,
a Mustang, five liter,
red, standard shift —
metal wings.

Coiled beside me test driving
he reins it back
on residential streets,
revving the engine: power,
throated, memorable
pulses through floorboard and seats.

He smiles
like a warrior anointed for battle,
a hand painted on his pony's rump,
eagle feathers in its mane.

From low knolls they watch us,
the selves we've left behind,
their war ponies pawing
dry tufts of grass.

We leave black marks,
soaring back to the dealership
in evening sun on vanquished prairie
and lightening bolts purged
from horses' thighs,

conquerors,
inheritors of fruits and spoils,
immortal on metal wings
through the gate at immaculate Ford,
revving the engine.

Trading Cars

On the showroom floor the Roadmaster is light blue with a darker blue interior. It's the first one of the new model I've seen. As the door opens the latch releases small, precise ticks. The dashboard sweeps across the car, deeper than a book shelf. The rear end and trunk stretch back to Uncle Joe's Hudson Hornet; the hood slopes toward infinity.

My hands appear small against the steering wheel, but I'm old enough to own this car. Quiet as a church, it swells with luxury and power.

"Bill," a voice whispers. I could have sworn it came from under the plush front seat, probably near the controls that move the seat up or down, forward or backward, or adjust the lumbar position to cradle your spinal curve.

"Bill," the voice comes again, this time from somewhere behind the shift indicator.

"Yes! I'm listening," I whisper, running my hand across the dash. The leather feels tight but soft. The controls just under the leather shelf are easy to see. They look important.

"Bill?" My wife's voice cuts like a fingernail across a blackboard. "What are you doing in there?" She's smiling, but her voice is sharp, almost accusatory, as though she's caught me in a compromising position. "R.G.'s ready," she tells me. He's the salesman, an older man with a diamond ring, who's about to lead us to the business manager, a man with two diamond rings. He'll finish the paperwork transferring us from our older, light blue LeSabre to the slightly used and smaller Century, a white one with spare trim.

I'll miss the LeSabre. I liked the name: *LeSabre, LeSabre* — "The vorpal blade went snicker-snack."

"Bill, come on," my wife calls. The door of the Roadmaster closes like I imagine the door on a bank vault closing.

"Nice, huh?" I'm nonchalant.

"Yes, Dear," my wife smiles. Walking just ahead of me down the hallway toward the business office she reminds me a little of my mother and the brisk way she used to walk as she pushed me in my perambulator, a purple one with cream trim and teardrop cowls over the swivel front wheels. A T-handle projected from a tray on the front, and a chromium rod curved around behind the front wheels to rest your feet on when you were being pushed. I liked that perambulator, especially when my mother disconnected the long handle from its slots in the rear and allowed me to walk the buggy around by myself.

On our way home we stop for a light at a major intersection at the foot of a low hill. An older man in dirty clothes and long overcoat waits beside several shopping bags filled with his belongings. My wife is reading the Owner's Manual; she likes to know where things are and glances now and then at the gauges and buttons on the dash.

The light takes a long time. The man glances at me, his unshaven face gaunt, spectral. He stares; our gazes lock. I nod and raise a couple of fingers briefly from the wheel. It's an acknowledgment, handed down from

primitive tribes, a modified gesture of the open hand —
I bear you no malice. I carry no weapons.

He does not respond, only stares as lines of traffic
move extra slowly across the complicated intersection
from different angles. I imagine for a moment that I've
seen this man some years before, somewhere — perhaps
camped on a highway island near the Cathedral of St.
Peter and St. Paul in Washington, D.C. I glance over at
him again through the open side window, His thinning
hair is uncombed, his coat hangs open and his khaki
pants bag around his dirty sneakers — a much older
man, I decide, and thinner.

He keeps staring as though sizing me up, looking
through the car. A young boy in a red Camaro appears in
my rearview mirror. He waits, rhythmically revving his
engine. His car rocks gently with the torque.

I courted my wife in a sixty-one Chevrolet Impala, a
Roman-red sports coupe with a 348 V-8 engine, white-
walled tires, fender skirts, dual exhausts, and two swept-
back aerials. I called it Big Red. "Man, when that car's
sitting still it looks like it's doing ninety-five," Steve
Frantz once told me.

We wait. The man keeps staring. It begins to drizzle,
and the light balking us reflects in the Century's white
hood. "It's used," I want to tell him, "my wife's car." He
doesn't move. I look away. It's early spring and the
dampness is chilly so I press the button and watch the
window climb noiselessly to the half-closed position.

The boy in the Camaro revs his engine, inching the
car forward then dropping back. The light changes. The
Camaro swerves quickly into the passing lane; its hood
jerks upward as the boy shifts to second gear. For a
moment I grip the steering wheel harder and press the

accelerator to the floor; the 3.3 liter, V-6 in the Century might handle the older Camaro, even with a 350 V-8, in a quarter mile.

"Bill!" My wife's voice comes from the other side of the car, quiet and cautionary like my mother's voice just before she snapped the handle back into the perambulator.

I ease up on the accelerator. In the rearview mirror I can still see the man standing in the center isle, watching as traffic swirls around him. The Camaro's hood jerks upward again as the boy shifts to high gear. He speeds past, the wash from his wheels misting through the half-open window and dampening the side of my face. I press the button on the arm rest; the window climbs to a fully-closed position. It's quiet inside.

The Camaro tops the hill, mist boiling from its wheels. It seems to hang for a moment before dropping out of sight, like one of those after-images you see when you close your eyes on a bright object.

My wife places the Owner's Manual back in the glove compartment. "I'm going to enjoy this car," she says. She runs her hand across the velour seat.

"Yeah," I reply. "It handles well; nice pickup." We don't say anything more. She smooths her skirt, folds her hands in her lap, and watches out the window. I ease up on the accelerator until the engine speed and road speed synchronize, then push the cruise control button and feel the subtle pulse as the mechanism takes over. The three shields in the round hood ornament glide above the right lane of the dual urban highway. Such a quiet, sedate car, comfortable and safe at just under fifty-five.